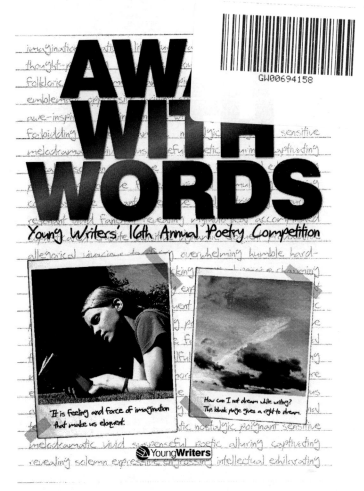

A WAY WITH WORDS

Young Writers' 16th Annual Poetry Competition

It is feeling and force of imagination that make us eloquent.

How can I not dream while writing? The blank page gives a right to dream.

Young**Writers**

West Country Verses
Edited by Claire Tupholme

 Young**Writers**

First published in Great Britain in 2007 by:
Young Writers
Remus House
Coltsfoot Drive
Peterborough
PE2 9JX
Telephone: 01733 890066
Website: www.youngwriters.co.uk

SB ISBN 978-1 84602 838 0

Foreword

This year, the Young Writers' *Away With Words* competition proudly presents a showcase of the best poetic talent selected from thousands of up-and-coming writers nationwide.

Young Writers was established in 1991 to promote the reading and writing of poetry within schools and to the young of today. Our books nurture and inspire confidence in the ability of young writers and provide a snapshot of poems written in schools and at home by budding poets of the future.

The thought, effort, imagination and hard work put into each poem impressed us all and the task of selecting poems was a difficult but nevertheless enjoyable experience.

We hope you are as pleased as we are with the final selection and that you and your family continue to be entertained with *Away With Words West Country Verses* for many years to come.

Contents

Stephanie Simmons (12)   22
Alison Hester (12)   23
Lucy Clayton (11)   24
Charlie Lapage-Norris (12)   24
Abbie Drew (11)   25
Lily Stalker (11)   25
Aifa Hart (11)   26
Jasmine Reiner (11)   27
Connor Morle (12)   28
Max Steadman (11)   29
Imogen Piper (11)   30
Oliver Morriss (11)   31
James Needham (14)   32
Cameron Passmore (11)   33
Charlie Gordon (11)   34
Oliver Seager (12)   35
Harry Bovington (11)   36
George Lunn (11)   36
Catherine Fielden (11)   37
Gemma Stevens (11)   37
Lauren Williams (11)   38
Tiffany Dike (11)   38
Ben Reiner (11)   39
Megan Archer (14)   39
Hannah Preece (13)   40
Beth Foye (12)   41
Frankie Luce (12)   41
Josh Close (14)   42
Sabina Grosch (12)   43
Becky Eastwood (12)   44
Hugh Bently (12)   44
Arizza Castalla (14)   45
Adam Waldron (14)   45
Kristian Cantle (12)   46
Adam Wykeham-Martin (14)   47
Jodie Watmore (12)   48

Cirencester Kingshill School, Cirencester

Tom Brown (13)   48
Amelia Nashe (14)   49
Tom Carter (13)   49

Edward Brown (13)	50
Sophie Russell (11)	50
Zoe Hollebon (12)	51
Jess Stockford (13)	51
Emma Benton (13)	52
Jade Smith (13)	52
Hannah Dawkins (13)	53
Emma Lambert (14)	53
Joseph Watkins (13)	54
James Freeman (13)	54
Matt Perry (13)	55
Tom Gardiner (12)	55
Loren Cowling (13)	56
Oliver Shurmer (13)	56
Sophie Benson (13)	57
Matt Berry (14)	57
Jenny Hayhurst (13)	58
Megan Tipper (12)	58
Beth Gray (13)	59
Charley Yates (12)	59
Ted Sales (13)	60
Natasha Taylor (14)	60
Georgina Shorter (13)	61
Charlie Walker (12)	61
Abby Wharton (13)	62
Georgina Gale (13)	62
Mollie Shute (12)	63
Laura Outram (12)	63
Johnathon Keary (12)	64
Chris Hasking (14)	65
Harriet Fox (12)	66
Matt Reynolds (13)	66
Nick Mellor (12)	67
Sebastian Johnson (13)	67
Tom Sutton (13)	68
Finlay Rochfort (13)	68
Alice Christopher (13)	69
Harriet Vickery (12)	69
Craig Aylett (13)	70
Ben Chapman (13)	70
Kirstie Jarvis (13)	71
Rachel Ody (13)	71

Zoe Shaw (13)	72
George Ford (12)	73
Alex Martin (13)	73
Jade Mathieson (12)	74
James Preston (12)	74
Emma Lawrence (12)	75
Charles Buse (12)	76
Max Clayton (12)	77
Mitch Potts (12)	78
Joanne Alderman (12)	78
Luke Oosthuizen (12)	79
Emma Legg (12)	79
Rebecca Hicks (12)	80
James O'Leary (12)	81
Rosie Mizon (12)	82
Rayner Killingback (11)	82
Emma Byrnes (13)	83
Coral Stratford-Smith (12)	84

Culverhay School, Bath

James Eynon (13)	85
Joe Payne (14)	86
Liam Hutchison (14)	87
Luke Taylor (14)	88
Steven Toogood (13)	89

Downend School, Bristol

Rebecca Whalley (14)	90
Sophie Chapman	91
Lauren Woodman (13)	92

Hayesfield School, Bath

Eleanor Child (12)	92
Claire Berrisford (12)	93
Ruth Byfield (12)	94
Annie Walker-Trafford (12)	94
Chelsea Buchan (12)	95
Adele Wills (12)	95
Sadie Thomas (11)	96
Freya Gill (11)	97
Tegan Pearce (12)	98

Stroud High School, Stroud

Lily Hughes (11)	123
Natasha Hole (11)	124
Megan Belcher (11)	125
Jessica Jackson (11)	126
Hannah Oulsnam (11)	126
Rebecca Field (11)	127
Robyn Overfield-Whitear (12)	128
Anne Townsend (11)	128
Holly Histed (11)	129
Cat Leach (11)	129
Georgia Saunders (11)	130
Alice Jollans (11)	131
Sophie Milner (11)	132
Esther Harding (14)	133
Annabel McCrindle (11)	134
Megan Jones (11)	135
Holly Davis-Grant (12)	136
Tabitha Haldane-Unwin (11)	137
Joanna Judd (12)	138
Danielle Munday (12)	139
Rachel Matthews (11)	140
Amy Watson (11)	141
Rebecca McKie (12)	142
Prudence Morgan-Wood (12)	143
Matilda McMorrow (11)	144
Amy Clark (11)	145
Holly Paveling (11)	146

The Crypt School, Gloucester

Liam Swattridge (13)	146
Luke Holbrook (14)	147
Sam Backhouse (14)	147
Mark Bates (14)	148
Ben Russell (11)	149
Matthew Gowell (15)	150
George Wright (14)	150
Martin Parker (14)	151
Kane Hazard (13)	151
James Keasley (13)	152
Stefan Quarry (14)	152

Wellsway School, Keynsham

Westonbirt School, Tetbury

The Poems

Into The Void

What lies ahead is hidden, what we leave behind is black,
We are hanging in the present, no way forward no way back.
Yet we keep pushing forward, we want to know what's there,
We bend over the precipice, into the dark we stare.

Because suspended in the present, we only glimpse what's here,
We have memories for survival and the future is unclear.
Where will we be going? Where will we have gone,
When the earth around us crumbles and the present has moved on?

Our buildings will crash down, mushroom clouds will fill the skies,
The lands will burst into flame, when our world dies.
We're lying to ourselves, we don't know where our road goes,
We're on the changing winds of time and we don't know
                                        where it blows.

We think we know it all, what a foolish race we are,
To believe we know every secret, and every shining star.
Why do we ask these questions? Will we ever know,
What is staring into us from the chasm far below?

Treasure every moment, or it will break like glass
Take a chance with destiny, before the moments pass.
You can try to shape your future, it is not set in stone.
Just don't lean too far over, you'll fall into the unknown.

So until it is the present, we should leave it alone,
Not ask any questions, not stray to the unknown.
It will come when it is ready, the climax of our climb,
The clashing bells of judgement day, the endless space of time.

Kate Chandler (15)
Bruton School for Girls, Bruton

Thief!

What isn't yours is taken,
What is has been mislaid.
The debtor's coming over,
He must be paid.

Ignore the soul inside you,
The Devil waits below.
God is Lord above you and
Your guilt will start to grow.

The ghoul outside the window
Is calling out your name.
Enquiring of your mother if
You wish to play a game.

He's standing on the doorstep,
He's calling out again.
He'll never leave the doorstep,
So never play the game!

Elena Barnard (14)
Bruton School for Girls, Bruton

The Seaside

To and fro went the waves,
As they crashed against the rocks and caves,
Children have fun,
Under the sun,
In the bouncing waves.

Fish and chips and candyfloss,
And the tourists' litter that they toss,
Is the seagulls unhealthy feast
And then are eaten by the shark,
'The Beast'.

Lauren Keylock (12)
Chosen Hill School, Churchdown

A Fig Tree

What would it be like to be a fig tree?
The hot spring Greek sun
Shining like a spotlight
With multiple earrings of juicy
Soft, tasty smooth figs.

My leaves are falling
Surely enough
I start to feel cold and bare
With a quilt of leaves gently lying at my base.

I'm bitterly cold with the
Whistling wind winding around
My bare stiff fingers
Stretched, reaching for the warmth
Of the earth.

I begin to sway to the slow
Rhythm of the spring spirit,
The warm comforting song
Of the sign of spring.

At last it's back and I
Start to put on my earrings
The sun is back to shine again
To show off my accessories.

A tall strong trunk
A twinkling rustle of leaves
The sweet songs of birds
Autumn, winter, spring and summer
The seasons pass
And it all starts again . . .

Alice King (12)
Chosen Hill School, Churchdown

Breaking Free

What happens when you meet in the most unlikely place?
Doing something you don't normally do.
Then you meet again by mistake,
And your world's turned upside-down.
What happens when rumours start to spread?
About how you met in the first place.
And they try to understand that you're not just a pretty face,
Or not just an extra piece in a puzzle.

The only opportunity to show yourself,
Is the school show.
In front of everyone . . .
Where it's all or nothing.
What happens when you get up on stage and freeze?
Not knowing what to do.
You look beside you and see your hero.
The one who's been there ever since you met.
The one who lifts you up when you're down.

You're scared . . .
You're anxious,
But you're there for a reason.
The piano has started,
Everyone is looking,
But you can't do it . . .
You don't want to make a fool of yourself,
But nothing's coming out your mouth.
You try and you try,
Finally your hero comes to the rescue.

'I can't do it,
Not with all these people watching.'
'I know you can,
Remember the night we met,
Just imagine we're there again.'
The conversation rings in my head,
Over and over again.
The piano starts again,
I hear his voice.

That wasn't the plan,
Then I remember why we're here . . .
To make a stand.
To break the stereotypes,
To stop jocks just being jocks,
And geeks just being geeks.

We were breaking free,
Breaking the mould.
Making everyone realise
That it was the start of something new.
We were showing the world who we were.

Once and for all.

Megan Hill (12)
Chosen Hill School, Churchdown

Homeless

His being is dampened and heavy,
In a bitter dark alley, below a dim lamp:
Its icy light, only hope it brings,
For there is no light in his blackened heart.
His body slumps low, in depressed sleep:
Like a black sun or a sea without salt.
No friend - but foe, he's accustomed to beating.
Not a life but a lonely soul;
His mind trails to the night he ran . . .
His frail, pale hand lifts for kindness:
Though passers-by stare or bark 'sorry,'
Not realising the sorrow which haunts him!
Grey clouds above, wind piercing, rain crashes,
Melting his empty body into numb: he quietly groans,
As he watches his life slowly, painfully wash away.

Stuart Perrett (13)
Chosen Hill School, Churchdown

The Big Bang!

I was all alone in empty space,
Until I saw a particle in the distance,
And to it I did race.

I was excited at the prospect of something new,
This place was so empty,
Silent too!

But before I could reach this tiny speck,
Came an almighty explosion,
And I thought, 'Oh Heck!'

As I felt in my throat the fear rise,
I couldn't help watching the once minuscule particle
Grow and grow and grow in size.

Much, much later, millions of years!
I came across a large lump of rock,
And said, 'What have I here?'

I called this rock Earth and today it still stands,
Much changed in form,
Across its lands.

Harriet Norfolk (12)
Chosen Hill School, Churchdown

Stranger

I'm walking round the edge of town,
So many strangers I can see,
But some of them are just my friends,
So they can't be strangers to me.

I'm walking round the centre of town,
I feel a little strange,
I swear there's someone following me,
But who could that person be?

I'm walking round the edge of town,
It's getting a little quieter,
I think I should go home now,
Because I'm getting a little whiter.

I'm walking round the top of my street,
Feeling a little scared,
Then someone grabbed me from behind,
And laughed a hee hee hee,
Then he whispered in my ear,
'I'm sorry I had to frighten you, but I think you lost your key,'
Then I turned around and saw that . . .
It was my dear friend Lee!

Shannon Page (12)
Chosen Hill School, Churchdown

Family

Family is always there,
There could never be too much of a family.
They do care.

They never stop loving you,
Even when you're dead.
But they will always be there,
Even when you go to bed.

When you are down,
They take care of you.
Help you to come around,
Even if your name is Sue.

If you are stuck,
All you need to do is yell.
But if you loved them back,
You'll never go to Hell.

So take care of your family,
Before they go.
But when you can't find them,
Then you will know.

Amie Trevarthen (12)
Chosen Hill School, Churchdown

Bubbles

As the sun goes down, and lights come alive,
His nose twitches and big black eyes shine.
He raids the food bowl, filling his pouches,
Hiding it secretly, in corners he crouches.

Then sitting on the bridge washing his little face,
And drinking noisily from the water bottle,
Squeaking on his wheel running round and round
At night in my house this is the only sound.

Kayleigh Askew (13)
Chosen Hill School, Churchdown

Nobody's There

I'm all alone
None to talk to or to tell

    Going to school
    Makes me worried, feeling scared.

      They make me feel so small,
      So tiny, so pathetic.

    Everything seems such a big deal
    Worried, I'll get something wrong to make
    Them come again.

They come at break, they come at lunch
Even outside my house.

Shouting, threatening
Hitting, kicking

    Nobody knows
    What happens behind these gates

      I'm all alone
      No one to talk to or to tell.

Flora Corbett (12)
Chosen Hill School, Churchdown

The Adelie Penguin

Adelie penguins are the smallest ones around,
Two feet tall, they only weigh nine pounds.

Tobogganing along the snow, moving quickly as they go,
Diving off cliffs and ice flows.

Seafood is delicious, fish their favourite food,
They dive down deep to find them in the oceans blue.

Their home is very chilly and to help them to stay warm,
They huddle together in a huge, enormous swarm.

Charles Simmonds (12)
Chosen Hill School, Churchdown

I Go There . . .

I go there twice a year,
It's one of my favourite places,
Candyfloss, ice cream, rides - the lot!
Lots of smiles on people's faces.

I go there for a daytrip,
To see the familiar things.
The tower, the circus and the lights,
And all the fun it brings!

I go there once a year,
It's my favourite campsite,
Swimming pools, ice cream, familiar faces,
And the brilliant sunsets at night.

I go there for two weeks,
I wish it could be longer!
Surfing the waves, cooling off in the sea,
As the sun gets stronger and stronger!

Ryan Greenwood (12)
Chosen Hill School, Churchdown

My Special Place

It can be dark and murky like a crisp cold winter's night.
It's peaceful like riding on a mast of a tall ship in the centre of a
                                        calm blue ocean.
You can feel the tickle of the wind beneath your bare feet.
You can hear the graceful birds singing in choirs flying above me.
You can see my visitors hopping about around me.
It's rich, bright, vivid and colourful.
Some days it's wet, like a cold day at a muddy beach.
Some days it's hot, like the hot, humid, sticky rainforest.
My special place is somewhere I can go when I feel upset, angry
                                        and distressed.
My special place is somewhere I can go to be by myself.

Mason Moore (12)
Chosen Hill School, Churchdown

Cycling Downhill

15, 16, 17, 18,
The speed dashes up,
My heart pumps rapidly,
Adrenaline kicks in!

19, 20, 21, 22,
I love the feeling,
Of carefree cycling.
Swift like a cheetah,
I persist down!

23, 24, 25, 26,
Hear the chain clicking,
Smell the oil,
Sense every bump and knock!

27, 28, 29, 30,
Now it's unsettling,
Losing stability;
Although excitement conquers!

29, 28, 27, 26,
The pace dives down,
The hill flattens out,
My energy sapped!

25, 24, 23, 22,
Now I'm bored,
No thrilling speed,
Or wind in my hair!

21, 20, 19, 18,
The downhill ride is over,
I think in my mind:
Do it again, do it again!

Christopher Perrett (13)
Chosen Hill School, Churchdown

Through The Eyes Of A Hero

I see a bright and promising future,
But this sight is far in the distance.
I must journey through this life to reach this goal,
This life will be hard and take its toll!
With both struggle through body and mind,
I will be able to reach and find this target.
To be able to climb the mountain of life,
It will take tremendous strength and might.
I am nearly at the top of this ladder of enlightenment,
I've nearly reached the hype and excitement.
I've made it to the top of the ladder, the peak of the mountain,
But now I must work even harder to stay here, keep my place.
My dream is now a reality,
I am now a famous and well loved celebrity.
Now I have new goals in life and am now facing another climb,
But I know I can make it because I've done it before!
And I will do it again!

Joshua Westcarr (12)
Chosen Hill School, Churchdown

The Unknown

Just off Florida, in the days of old
When the storms were raging and the seas cold.
The pilots and captains did their best
To keep the crew's mind at rest.

Their minds and hearts were full of fear
For many a boat and aircraft would disappear.
You approach the place from any angle
The place of course is the
Bermuda Triangle.

The explanation people endeavour
Like men of old they blamed the weather
But the weather was not *all* of course
It was the thing you call the
Magnetic force.

Nathan Littler (11)
Cirencester Deer Park School, Cirencester

If I Could Stop The Clocks . . .

If I could stop the clocks,
I would make the boys wear the frocks.
If I could stop the clocks,
I would make Tony Blair wear smelly socks.
This would be my dream, my one and only dream.

If I could stop the clocks,
I would stop the disasters and the mocks.
If I could stop the clocks,
I would get a boat and sail from the docks.
This would be my dream, my one and only dream.

If I could stop the clocks I'd be a,
Miracle maker.
If I I did stop the clocks I'd be a
Genius.

Molly Stooke (12)
Cirencester Deer Park School, Cirencester

Into The Unknown

I'm falling,
Falling upward,
I see hippopotamuses in tutus leaping, pirouetting and
Prancing gracefully in circular precession,
I see waves of crisp golden corn being steadily flattened by
An elusive UFO
I see an ugly, green wrinkly being leap out angrily and aim a decrepit
Looking gun in my direction,
I see purple authoritative walruses hurling gambling
Chips and playing poker,
Suddenly the whole picture shatters and implodes into tiny fragments,
Had the whole world gone mad,
More to the point,
Had I?

Ben Chadwick (12)
Cirencester Deer Park School, Cirencester

My Hero Jimi Hendrix

His music is unique to him in every way,
For his 1st guitar it was $5 to pay.
1969 was his best year
But bad things were round the corner to fear.

On the 18th of September he passed away,
He has been remembered till this day.
Sadly it was a miserable end,
Let's face it he was a guitar legend.

He has been considered the king of guitar,
He was applauded for music considered bizarre.
The way he plays his guitar inspires me,
To rock all night till half-past three.

He loved playing on his Fender guitar,
He loved what he did being a rock star!
I wish I was there to see him succeed,
From the guy at the back to the guy on lead!

His music has changed me in many ways,
I give his music all my praise.
He was a genius, considered a poet,
Though at times he did not know it.

I hope you have all listened to at least one song,
Because I could hear them all day long.
If you have not, I urge you do,
As he could inspire you!

Elli Clark (12)
Cirencester Deer Park School, Cirencester

Stop The Clocks

Stop the clocks, stop everyone fighting
For just a single second, stop everything bad
Stop the clocks, make everyone calm
Give them time to reflect on the good times they've had.

Stop the clocks, stop everyone moving
Just for a bit, just a little while
Stop the clocks; give them all a minute of rest
Stop them from frowning, let them all smile.

Stop the clocks, give them sweet warm silence
Only for a short time, let it hang in the air
Stop the clocks; let them listen to the peace
Watch the frozen chaos and feel the wind in their hair.

Stop the clocks, stop time running ever forward
A lightning fast beast stopping for no one
Stop the clocks, put a pause on life
Give us all time to look and think about what we've done.

Stop the clocks, for me to come and find you
Just to be with you not for long
Stop the clocks, give us time together
While all others are stopped give us time to belong.

Stop the clocks, for me to come and see you
We can laugh till we cry it'll all be good fun
Stop the clocks, for a time without family or distraction
Come on, the good times have only just begun!

Rachel King (13)
Cirencester Deer Park School, Cirencester

Murder Mystery Poem

You hear a police car in distant sound
Only hear it you do not see
It fades away into silent ground
Like the person who was standing next to me.

Don't go to the past running around
You'll put a hold on life
If you go you will be found
Though you may encounter a knife.

You secretly hide from someone not there
Just remember it's all in your head
You try to hurt someone but you wouldn't dare
Till you realise you're the one who's dead.

You see a light, first dim then bright
It leads you unwillingly forward
Deep in the night you're in for a fright
I know I wouldn't dare but you would.

Zoe Pearce (12)
Cirencester Deer Park School, Cirencester

My Hero

50 Cent is me hero
I like to drink lots of Coca-Cola Zero
I carry a pistol in my pocket
And I attach kids' soldiers to a rocket
Me best mate is Eminem
And I like to eat M & Ms
Yesterday I got in a fight
After that I got a pint
I like to wear me homie bandana
When I get home I'm a bit of a spanner
This is the end of me rap
Coz I'm going to have a nap.

Kieren Knowles (11)
Cirencester Deer Park School, Cirencester

A Way With Words

If I had all the words in the world
I would use but just a few
And make my own new language
That was easy for me and you.

Every word would be easy to spell
So writing wouldn't go wrong
Reading out loud would be a joy
I might just do it all in song.

No more C grades for my spelling
No more red marks in my book
When my teacher asks if work is done
I'll say why don't you take a look!

The new language would be simple
Just as easy for he or she
So great would be my invention
I might just keep it all for me!

Matthew George (11)
Cirencester Deer Park School, Cirencester

Stop The Clocks

Time has frozen still,
It cannot go forward,
And it cannot go back,
No one can enter the world,
And no one can leave,
No one can carry on with their life . . .

Time has frozen still,
The watch stopped ticking,
And the grandfather clock,
Stopped chiming,
No one can smile,
And no one can shed tears.

Lucy Reeves (11)
Cirencester Deer Park School, Cirencester

My Hero - Beth

My hero Beth,
She isn't scared of death!

Her best friend is Jen
Who has a colourful pen!

She is as beautiful as a rose
But she cannot do a pose!

Her favourite band is 'System of a Down'
She's funny because she will never frown!

Beth is bright, Beth is the sun,
Beth is a person who loves everyone!

Beth is very very nice
Although she won't eat rice!

She isn't scared of death
My hero Beth.

Guy Ody (12)
Cirencester Deer Park School, Cirencester

Stop The Clocks

Stop the clocks, time moves on,
Let me go back, have another chance.
As I go on let me breathe,
Let me go back and dance.

The air flows on like a rushing river,
Running down the side.
Nothing good, nothing bad,
Time moves on like it's sad.

Stop the clocks, time moves on,
Let me go back, have another chance.
As I go on let me breathe,
Let me go back and dance.

Emma Spring (11)
Cirencester Deer Park School, Cirencester

And Into The Unknown

The black hole stood, a gigantic vacuum in deep space.
I floated a mile or so off,
It tempted me to fly closer, and be sucked into the swirling vortex,
And into the unknown.

But then I brought myself back to reality,
This small cargo carrier would be torn to pieces by pressure.
I sat, weighing up my odds,
Into the unknown.

An hour passed, I'd made up my decision,
Though I still had doubts,
But I was going to do it, despite my cowardly conscience,
Earth contacted me, trying to get me to change my mind,
But there was nothing to go back to, only war, pollution and crime.
I opened up the throttle,

And into the unknown.

Dominic Brown (12)
Cirencester Deer Park School, Cirencester

My Hero

My main hero is Girls Aloud,
They sing my favourite songs and make me sing out loud.

Their songs are so great, I stay up so late
Listening to their songs, in the mornings I feel so wrong.

Their albums are trendy, says my mate Wendy.

At singing they're the greatest yet,
I have some of their CDs, how many can I get?

In my eyes they are the best
Better than the rest.

Their albums are so funky,
Their population is so chunky.

They are my hero,
All the rest are zero.

Phoebe Somers (11)
Cirencester Deer Park School, Cirencester

Stop The Clocks!

The clocks have stopped
Everything and everyone
Is still, apart from me.
I walk through the park
The sound of my feet touching the ground echoes
People everywhere
A frisbee in mid-air
But no life anywhere
Through the dead quiet park I walk on.

The river that used to rush and roar is lifeless
The chattering children in the playground have frozen
The trees in the wood that would swing and sway are silent
I walk on.

I peer through windows and see families gathered
With a gorgeous food layout on the table
With people in a chomping motion
Smiles are stuck on people's faces.

The clocks have stopped
There's no going forward
There's no going back
Just trapped in time
The clocks have stopped.

Megan Hargreaves (11)
Cirencester Deer Park School, Cirencester

Flintoff

F antastic at cricket
L asting team spirit
I n good form
N ever out of energy
T ough
O ver the game like he controls it
F lowing confidence all the time
F abulous all-rounder.

Jack Hannam (12)
Cirencester Deer Park School, Cirencester

A Way With Words

There once was a girl, who couldn't stop talking,
They gagged her and tied her but she kept on squawking.

Once came the day when she finally got free,
She jumped up and down and screamed, 'Yippee!'

She went to the church and shouted loudly,
'I am the best!' She said ever so proudly.

She went to the shop to show off her vocabulary,
She came out with some gum that she bought rarely.

She started to chew on the gum that she bought,
'This tastes disgusting,' she said, distraught.

He went to change it, and he gave her a choice,
She went to say blue but lost her voice.

She ran straight home to tell her dad,
He was pleased but still felt bad.

That was the girl who wouldn't stop talking,
What about you? Are you still talking?

Steph Hacker (11)
Cirencester Deer Park School, Cirencester

Where And What's The Unknown

Go to places unknown
Go to the centre of the universe
But don't become alone
Be the unraveller of a curse
Travel into the unknown.

Be the unexplored map
Begin your world whenever
Go to where happiness is on tap
Just don't forget to be clever
Travel into the unknown.

You can do it
If you put your mind to it.

Charlotte Saunders (11)
Cirencester Deer Park School, Cirencester

The Frozen World

The clocks have stopped,
Cars have halted,
Planes in midflight,
Nothing moves in the frozen.

The clocks have stopped,
In mid movement people frozen,
The chaffinch's song hangs in the air,
Nothing moves in the frozen.

The clocks have stopped,
Woodcutter's axe suspended in time,
The woodcutter's hand gripping the handle,
With his arms in a permanent flex,
Nothing moves in the frozen.

The clocks have stops,
When there are people frozen,
Cars halted,
Planes in midflight,
Birds' songs in the air,
When nothing moved in the frozen . . .

Miles Jarvis (11)
Cirencester Deer Park School, Cirencester

A Way With Words

As I lie in bed I think of you
As I look in your empty place in bed
Where did I leave you?
Where did you go?
Are you out in the rain wandering all alone
When you could be in the warm at home with me in bed
You are warm and cuddly
You are the best teddy bear in the world.

Stephanie Simmons (12)
Cirencester Deer Park School, Cirencester

All Because Of You

In the jungle lives
The big chest-hitting gorillas
But how long will we see them living there for?
For all the trees are being cut down
All because of you.

In the Arctic lives
The snow-white polar bears
But how long will we see them living there for?
For the ice is melting away
All because of you.

In the ocean lives
The mighty blue whales
But how long will we see them living there for?
For the ocean is being polluted
All because of you.

In the jungle lives
The chirping rainbow parrots
But how long will we see them living there for?
For their homes are being destroyed
All because of you.

In the Arctic lives
The sleek shiny seals
But how long will we see them living there for?
For their food is being poisoned
All because of you.

In the ocean lives
The colourful clownfish
But how long will we see them living there for?
For the plants are dying out
All because of you.

In the houses live
The pollution makers
But how long will we live for?
For we are killing ourselves
All because of us!

Alison Hester (12)
Cirencester Deer Park School, Cirencester

Stop The Clocks

Time is still
Death is near
So many things I cannot redo
I cannot go forwards
I cannot go back
What have I done?
Stop the clocks.

What can I do?
Where am I?
So many things I cannot redo
Such a long way
Please let me back
What have I done?
Stop the clocks.

I am so scared
Worried and petrified
So many things I cannot redo
Go tell the angels I'll change my ways
What have I done?
Stop the clocks.

Lucy Clayton (11)
Cirencester Deer Park School, Cirencester

Through The Future

James go and tidy your room,
Yes Mum, of course . . . Mu . . .
And the house fell silent,
All apart from the tick-tock, tick-tock
Of James' grandfather's pocket watch in James' hand.

Then it happened, the hands on the clock,
Began to spin still keeping up the faint
Tick-tock, tick-tock,
And then the room began to spin as well,
Faster, faster, faster, fas . . .

Charlie Lapage-Norris (12)
Cirencester Deer Park School, Cirencester

Into The Unknown

My dog's bedroom is such a mess,
You don't know where you are,
If you're even in there, it's like being
In a smashed-up car,
When he eats,
It's like a warthog,
And he's always as bouncy as a frog,
He's sometimes calm,
But never harmed.

My dog is sometimes naughty,
He'll live till probably forty.
When he's ill,
He always will,
Get the fuss,
Get the treats,
And get everything for weeks and weeks.
My dog is the cutest,
That will never be beaten!
My dog is such a sweetheart!
He's always in my heart!

Abbie Drew (11)
Cirencester Deer Park School, Cirencester

Stop The Clocks

Stop the clocks.
This night is magical and I don't want to waste it.
I don't want this night to end.
I wish I could stay here forever
Stop the winds from blowing
Stop the birds from singing
And stop everyone from moving
Just let me stay here forever . . .

Lily Stalker (11)
Cirencester Deer Park School, Cirencester

The Day Of The Dead!

H allowe'en is a time for ghosts and ghouls to come to Earth
   To celebrate their one day of torture.
A lways they are watching, always they are waiting
   For the day to come.
L ove is not an option on Hallowe'en
   The only people allowed are people who are frightened,
   Nervous or shy.
L et us celebrate the day of the dead with the spirits,
   Poltergeists and phantoms
O r they will come for us, torture us.
W ords, three of them represent Hallowe'en: Trick or Treat!
E ver ignore these words and children dress up and act for the
   Sun, the moon and middle Earth
E ven if you are the world's nicest people, they will throw eggs
   At your perfect house.
   If you want to stop this give them treats.
   Lots of treats and you will be safe.
N ever underestimate the power of Hell because they could just
   As easily sneak up on you.

Aifa Hart (11)
Cirencester Deer Park School, Cirencester

Stop The Clocks

Stop the clocks, it's time to end, things have stopped, no more
will happen.
Stop the clocks, people, places, none will change or get old.
Stop the clocks, no more will the sunrise or the moon light up the sky.
Stop the clocks, summer, autumn, winter and spring will
not happen again.
Stop the clocks, the song has carried on running through,
Time will travel no more.
Stop the clocks, places that are lost will never be found.
Stop the clocks, hate and sadness have stopped, tears will never
fall again.
Stop the clocks, animal species will not die.
Stop the clocks, things that must be done, time will never run
out to do them.
Stop the clocks, just like shops, the shelves will never get empty.
Stop the clocks the rivers, streams and seas will never run dry.
Stop the clocks, ideas, things will not change or make a move.
Stop the clocks, people say time is precious, but now it can never
be wasted.

Jasmine Reiner (11)
Cirencester Deer Park School, Cirencester

Stop The Clocks

Silence . . .
Silence like the wind,
Silence echoing through me and the world around me,
Silence booming in my ears,
Silence in this dead world,
Silence I cannot help but notice . . .

Stillness . . .
Stillness as though nothing could be bothered to move,
As though there was no need to,
Still as a corpse,
Still as a rock,
Stillness in this dead world,
Stillness that my body is eager to betray . . .

Nothing could live here,
What would want to?
What kind of creature would live here?
In this lonely, evil place,
With the timeless Earth,
With the silent wind,
With the deadly sun,
And lack of water,
It lives up to its name,
As well as it would be possible,
Death Valley.

Connor Morle (12)
Cirencester Deer Park School, Cirencester

The Dream

Wear the kit of Liverpool,
Feel the red fabric against your skin,
Look around and see your teammates excited,
Focused.
You all know this is the most important game.
Win it and the FA Cup is yours
Glory and pride filling your soul.

You step out of the changing room.
Chelsea are already there staring straight ahead.
I see Terry wearing the captain's armband.
Today I could be the captain for Liverpool.
I step out onto the pitch.
The flashlights are on, cameras are flashing,
Fans are cheering,
The whistle blows.

This is it the penalty that will decide the game.
I step up.
I kick.
Goal.
Fans roar with happiness.
The cup is in my hands.
I lift the cup.
My teammates surround me.
Glory fills our souls.
The prize is ours,
The dream is lived.

Max Steadman (11)
Cirencester Deer Park School, Cirencester

Into The Unknown . . .

As I looked out of my window, I saw a bird then the sky,
The blanket of the Earth,
Warming it and protecting it.
I saw a flock of birds soaring up high and I said,
'I wish I could be like that, wandering the great outdoors
Without a care in the world.'

When I say this for the third time I find myself floating and
Beginning to grow wings, golden ones.
I start to flap them and as I think all my thoughts float
Around me even the most extraordinary ones.

When I start to move my thoughts travel with me,
I get confused and decide to look beneath me.
My mum always told me people look like ants from above
But she must be wrong as there is no one there,
I start to picture my gran and from out of nowhere there she is.

I then see that when I think of something it appears.
I then see all my thoughts trapping me and the only way to
Escape is to clear my mind.

I start to try and think of nothing, but then I am still thinking of
Something: Nothing!
I then realised that I would have to really believe that I was
Something else I did and pictured myself as that little bird
                                        on my window.

And that is how me, Imogen, became one of the beautiful things
In the universe, something I have always wanted to be . . .

                        . . . at peace with myself.

Imogen Piper (11)
Cirencester Deer Park School, Cirencester

The Place Of The Unknowns

As I stand at the edge of the chasm I wonder . . .
I wonder about everything that is unknown to me,
Thoughts of things I don't know crowd into my mind,
For this is the place of the unknowns.

As I descend into the chasm I wonder . . .
What is ahead of me,
What is down here,
In this place of the unknowns.

As I reach the bottom I wonder . . .
What is along this tunnel,
What is that noise,
Down in this place of the unknowns.

I see all the unknowns crowded in this cavern and I wonder . . .
When will they be found,
Or will they be trapped here forever,
Alone in the place of the unknowns.

I feel sorry for them so I grab them and throw them out
across the world,
And I wonder . . .
What more can people know now that all the unknowns are gone,
Now there's nothing in the place of the unknowns.

I see unknowns growing . . .
And I smile.

Oliver Morriss (11)
Cirencester Deer Park School, Cirencester

Into The Unknown

I left everything behind
I left my friends, my house, my bed, my family
Everything that meant something I had left back where I had
come from

I was walking down a dark cold street
I was all alone; I was scared, cold, hungry and lonely
I had nowhere to go
I don't remember now why I ran away
I left everything I love and know
I was lost in an alleyway only 100 yards long
I was lost in my head, my mind, my head was wrong
Running from nothing and no one
I changed my mind
I want to go home, I've had enough
No one could hear me even if I screamed
I was in the unknown
I was trapped and scared
I couldn't escape
There's nowhere to go
I am sorry I want to come home!

James Needham (14)
Cirencester Deer Park School, Cirencester

If I Could Read Minds

If I could read minds,
I would rule the world,
I could see if people were innocent.

If I could read minds,
I would see what people are thinking
I could see if people were guilty.

If I could read minds,
I would see what people are going to do next,
I could be king of the universe.

If I could read minds,
I would know what animals are thinking,
I could rule the animal kingdom.

If I could read minds,
I would see if people were troubled,
I could help anyone in the world,

If I could read minds,
I would learn about the world,
I could teach people better.

Cameron Passmore (11)
Cirencester Deer Park School, Cirencester

Stop The Clock - Playing Rugby For Gloucester And For England

I can only dream of wearing that shirt
I can only dream of what that must feel like - to have achieved
Your dream - but the clock has stopped and the moment is mine.

Kingsholme Stadium is large and green - the posts stand tall at
                                                    either end.
Every place in the sheds and the stands is taken
Today will be my day.

I step out onto the pitch - my heart is thumping fast
I am fly-half and the pressure is on
Today we must win.

The teams stand opposite each other
The whistle goes by the French ref - this is it!
Tactics-pass, tackle, remember we can *win*.

Two minutes to go
Yes I score the final try
It is over
The crowd is going wild
I feel the heat from them - from me.

We have won
I am the hero that I dream about being.

Charlie Gordon (11)
Cirencester Deer Park School, Cirencester

My Hero

My hero is yet to be a star,
He's my hero cos of how he got this far.
He started his football career at Yeading,
For his great first touch and powerful heading
A nobody
He inspired his team to a great FA Cup,
Only against Newcastle would they trip up.
A local star
League Two Brentford moved in for the buy,
And from then on his career would fly
A pro new boy
The FA Cup did him wonders again,
Only in the fifth round brave Brentford would end.
A rediscovered hero
This great story moved to the English top flight,
And Steve Bruce described him as 'The next Ian Wright'.
A new prospect
But tragedy struck as Newcastle returned,
The Brummies went down and the lesson was learned.
A chance
Star-striker Heskey moved on from the side,
And then his first goal to the net it would glide.
A true Brummie
A move back to the Prem could make him a star,
It's now up to him if he gets that far.

Oliver Seager (12)
Cirencester Deer Park School, Cirencester

Into The Unknown

The unknown as one, is like a fort
A bedsheet held up,
Flat and taut
Can be penetrated
But hard to expose,
For all who try come
Few highs, many lows.

Brutal it can be or renowned
Through a lie, like trying to read,
When blind in one eye.
Looking for unknown,
That's more than just Earth,
Is not really essential,
But an instinct of birth.

Mysteries of the past and the future, still
The unknown will always be linked to God's will.

Harry Bovington (11)
Cirencester Deer Park School, Cirencester

Stop The Clocks

S top the clocks the wizard chanted
T he entire time continuum stopped in its tracks
O nly one thing was left moving, the time wizard
P ouring rain had stopped falling.

T he lightning was a still flash in the air.
H orribly loud thunder was nothing but silence.
E verything was frozen.

C louds were as still as a dead ghost
L orries and cars looked like they were parked in the road.
O nly the time wizard could change all this.
C locks everywhere had stopped ticking.
K ings of everything cannot do what the wizard has.
S omehow the time wizard has done all this.

George Lunn (11)
Cirencester Deer Park School, Cirencester

What Do Babies Think?

What do babies think,
When they come on out?
What do they think,
When they scream and shout?

What do they think,
When their mums come running?
What do they think,
When their dad tries to do the plumbing!

What do they think,
When they see all the toys?
What do they think,
If they are boys?

What do babies think,
When they chew their toe?
What do they think,
I guess we'll never know!

Catherine Fielden (11)
Cirencester Deer Park School, Cirencester

Stop The Clocks

If I could stop the clocks, I'd . . .
Bungee-jump off a plane,
I'd eat the world's largest candy cane.
Sail down Niagara Falls
And go to all the shopping malls.

I'd love to drive a Formula One car and
Play the electric guitar.
I would also like to meet Johnny Depp,
Being his wife would be the next step!

Flying to the moon would be fun
And so would lying on a beach catching sun.
My last wish would be to star in my own TV show
And go skiing in the snow!

Gemma Stevens (11)
Cirencester Deer Park School, Cirencester

Stop The Clocks

What would happen if the clocks stopped . . .
Would there be money to nick
Or free lollies to lick?
Time to travel far
Or buy a new car?
Time to go to New Delhi
Or eat ten plates of jelly?
Ride a camel in the Sahara
Or try the Queen's tiara?
Go to the Pyrenees
Or have tea with chimpanzees?
Visit Santa at the North Pole
Or for England score a goal?
Buy clothes in Paris or Milan
Or lie on the beach and get a tan?
Ride on a yak
And when you get back
Pretend you've been nowhere at all.

Lauren Williams (11)
Cirencester Deer Park School, Cirencester

My Hero

Superstars of films
Lots of fun and laughter wherever they are
Their plots are sometimes crazy, full of excitement and glee
There's always a happy ending we will agree
They both have passion for fashion
And enjoy dressing up
They will always be together, they will never break up
They're both very sporty
And can be very, very naughty
Always being on the good side
They'll always have a charming side
They travel the world far and wide
They are never on their own but side by side.

Tiffany Dike (11)
Cirencester Deer Park School, Cirencester

Into The Unknown

Am I flying? No falling, into the unknown,
Plunging down into the steamy abyss below,
Flying fast in the celestial void of space,
Falling, falling down and down, spinning and turning.

As I tumble over and over, crashing and spinning
                                out of the atmosphere,
Falling and flying at the same time, gliding through
                                the highest clouds,
Higher than the stars in the furthest galaxies of the
                                strangest universes,
The breeze blowing around me, lifting me higher and keeping
                                                me going.

Through the void, nothing exists neither does time exist or pass,
Through the void, no seasons are there, no days or weeks,
                                no months or years,
Through the void, through the void, through the void . . .

Ben Reiner (11)
Cirencester Deer Park School, Cirencester

Stop The Clocks

Everything is gleaming
The snow lies on the hill
The pond is ice and sparkling
It all just looks so still.

The trees are glistening slightly
Crusted and gleaming with frost
The flower beds are hidden
Lonely, cold and lost.

The icicles are shimmering
Snow glistening on the rocks
Everything is frozen
The snow has stopped the clocks.

Megan Archer (14)
Cirencester Deer Park School, Cirencester

Turn Back The Clock

Turn back the clock
Until I say stop.
Guy Fawkes, treason and plot.
And travel through time
In a Roman straight line
Adam, Caesar - the lot.

First pre-historic ages
Before there were wages
And the Earth was bubbly hot
Then the caveman era
Evolution got nearer
Standing more upright than not.

Jumping along
Humankind going strong
King Harold was fighting a lot.
An arrow through the eye
He would do nothing but cry
Shortly after, he lost the plot.

From that to Cromwell
Revolution raised hell
And Charles did diddly-squat.
Ollie chopped off his head
And left him for dead
Then went and did - not a lot.

World War 1 and then II
With Hitler hating the Jews
Six years before Churchill said, 'Stop!'
With a cigar in his hand
He took a firm stand
With our great grandparents - they gave us their lot.

So that's crystal clear
How we ended up here
And we are grateful for what we have got
But now it is time
To finish this rhyme
The end, goodbye, full stop.

Hannah Preece (13)
Cirencester Deer Park School, Cirencester

My Hero Guy

Guy has got hair as curly as a spring,
And it looks so funny when it's as straight as a pin.

Guy is bright, Guy is the sun,
Guy is caring and loves everyone.

Guy is an angel; he gives a golden glow,
Guy is like one big freak show.

Guy is as tall as the tallest trees,
Guy makes small people look like fleas.

Guy can sometimes be very rude,
But Guy is really a very cool dude.

Guy is silly, Guy is fun,
When he tickles me, I laugh a tonne.

Beth Foye (12)
Cirencester Deer Park School, Cirencester

If I Could Stop Clocks!

If I could stop the clocks
I would make the boys wear the frocks,
If I could stop the clock
I would make Tony Blair wear smelly socks,
This would be my dream my one and only dream.

If I could stop the clocks
I would stop the disasters and the mocks,
If I could stop the clocks
I would destroy all the old smocks
If I could stop the clocks
I would lock all the ships in the dock.
If I could stop the clocks
I would lock Jordan in with lots of smelly sheep and their flock!
This would be my dream my one and only dream.

Frankie Luce (12)
Cirencester Deer Park School, Cirencester

Into The Unknown

The sleek white pristine walls,
Men in black and white suits,
Guns, weapons and gadgets,
All of this is in the unknown,
And the people should be unheard of.
Desks lined with computers,
Crunching through meaningless code,
All of this I will never know,
In the unknown.

Further into the building,
More of this I will have never seen,
If asked I don't know,
For all of this is secret and unheard of.
'Top Secret' the documents say,
If I was to read it,
Or leave it,
I still don't know what is in there.
In the unknown.

In my office,
The same white walls cleaned to perfection,
A computer on my desk,
A report on the recent events around the world,
All of this you will never have heard of,
Though I haven't heard of this either,
In the unknown.

Josh Close (14)
Cirencester Deer Park School, Cirencester

Aliens Steal From The Sweet Shop

A spaceship landed in my street,
It was blue with silver lights,
I watched as the small door opened,
It was quite a spectacular sight.
Out hopped a small red creature,
With three arms and just one eye,
It had six legs but only two toes
And it looked extremely sly.
Another alien came out of the spaceship,
Carefully looking around,
The aliens were very cautious
And they didn't make a sound.
Lots more red aliens followed on,
Carrying huge brown sacks,
They headed towards the town,
Leaving crumbs to retrace their tracks.
A little while later they returned,
Their sacks full to the top,
They all climbed back into their spaceship,
Sweeping up the crumbs with a mop.
They closed the small door silently,
Leaving no traces at all,
They took off for their home in space,
I thought it was really cool.
I had no idea what they'd taken,
But the newspaper told me right,
'Sweet shop left with no sweets,
From robbery last night'!

Sabina Grosch (12)
Cirencester Deer Park School, Cirencester

Stop The Clocks

Stop the clocks,
Go forward in time,
Flying cars
And one is mine.

Me in the future,
At 21,
I have my own house
How much fun.

My job is a teacher,
I work at Stratton,
Everything's fine,
Until I teach Latin.

My fantastic journey,
Is coming to an end,
I must go,
And make amends.

Becky Eastwood (12)
Cirencester Deer Park School, Cirencester

My Hero

He picks up the ball on the edge of the area,
Shoots . . .
The net billows,
Crowd jumps up in joy,
Shearer! Shearer!
They roar,
It echoes around the stands,
He runs to the edge of the pitch,
Raises his fist in delight,
As the crowd roar even more.
That is why he is my hero.
Shooting,
And scoring.

Hugh Bently (12)
Cirencester Deer Park School, Cirencester

Into The Unknown

Why do stars fade their light?
Does the moon in the sky lose its side?
For you the world maybe flicker in flight
Come a little closer
Into the unknown
Don't you wash away that smile?
Just look away and
Freeze in the sun
Burn in the rain
I don't care what they say
I don't care what they do
'Cause in this vacuous night
We'll leave our fears behind
Continue our journey
And I will never let go
Into the unknown.

Arizza Castalla (14)
Cirencester Deer Park School, Cirencester

Stop The Clocks

Tick-tick, tick-tock,
The clock never stops,
Every tick the world becomes more unfit,
Pollution everywhere, forests looking bare,
No time to spare,
We need to stop and clear up, but nobody seems to care,
All wrapped up in their own little world,
Theirs isn't bare,
So why should they care,
One big time bomb waiting for the last tock,
Just another car journey decreasing the tick-tocks,
Just another load of ticks gone,
Just waiting for death, who cares you're the best,
Have us dying on your chest, stop,
Tick-tock, tick-tock.

Adam Waldron (14)
Cirencester Deer Park School, Cirencester

One Man, One Desire

One man one desire
He goes into another dimension
And his eyes are on fire

He tries to go home but
He's on his own
He thinks he's OK
But he's really all alone

The clocks have moved on
And he can't go back
He feels like he's lost
And frightened to look back

He thinks it's a nightmare
He thinks it will end
But the hole that he tore
Will never mend.

His hands are trembling
Trembling with fear
He can hear the owls
Hooting in his ear.

Kristian Cantle (12)
Cirencester Deer Park School, Cirencester

Secret Service - Into The Unknown

The unknown secret service plane,
Filled with gadgets, filled with guns,
Almost invisible to the human eye,
Every panel a jaunty angle,
Fast as a cheetah, striking through the air,
Flies so high, you don't even know.

The secret service plane into the unknown,
The dark, distant galaxy,
Asteroids ascending in the atmosphere,
The lights on the plane glowing
Lighting up the black expanse.

The secret service plane in the unknown,
Boom, bash, clang,
The bulk of rock impacting on the plane,
Just bouncing back off like springs,
Back into existence,
It had landed,
But still nobody saw,
It was the unknown,
The secret service plane.

Adam Wykeham-Martin (14)
Cirencester Deer Park School, Cirencester

What Would I Do?

If I stopped a clock,
I wouldn't know what to do.
Would I climb a building
Or make my dreams come true?

I have crazy ideas,
Which ones should I choose?
Would I buy some cakes
Or wear lots and lots of shoes?

Would I draw on faces?
Would I climb up walls?
Would I jump around places
Or go to shopping malls?

Maybe I'll just stay in class,
But OK one more wish.
Are you ready everyone?
I wish I was a fish.

Jodie Watmore (12)
Cirencester Deer Park School, Cirencester

Cars

They are very good
Under the hood.
They are fast
Like a blast.
They are colourful
They are wonderful!
I am in my car
And I am going far!
I am going to see Ann
To drink a Coke can,
I am going to drink some beer,
I am going to the pier!

Tom Brown (13)
Cirencester Kingshill School, Cirencester

One In Millions

They're running forward fast,
Five hundred men
Hearts beating, sweaty hands,
In a parody race to live.

Silver monsters of barbed wire
Rise up against them.
Most men make it past
But one in millions falls.

A bullet to the chest, a bullet to the leg,
As he lies in the mud
In his own pool of blood,
He watches friends run past, no longer is he in the race.

As his world goes red, and with his dying breath
He protests silently, 'Why oh why
Did it have to be me?'

He was just one, just one of the millions
Who died in vain, no one to ease their pain.

Amelia Nashe (14)
Cirencester Kingshill School, Cirencester

Homeless Poem

No comfort where I lay
No warmth where I stay
No bills to pay.

I have cold feet
I have nothing to eat
I have no one to meet.

I have nowhere to camp
I am just a smelly old tramp
And my bottom is getting damp.

Tom Carter (13)
Cirencester Kingshill School, Cirencester

The Ghosts Of The Streets

We are the ghosts of the streets
Dreaming of tenderest meats
We just lay there covered in dirt
Always hungry or hurt.

A stranger's walking by
With his posh fancy new tie
I asked him for some money
He said, 'You trying to be funny?'

Night was coming fast
But people were still walking past
I started to look for a doorway
Where I can rest and lay.

Just like I said
It is like we do not need to be fed
Or we have no feelings too
They just stare and think *who are you?*

The common people take away our belief
Sometimes we have to walk miles to get some relief
We have to beg for money or rot
Then you get knifed or shot.

Edward Brown (13)
Cirencester Kingshill School, Cirencester

Happy Days

Mondays are magical,
Tuesdays are terrific,
Wednesday is wicked,
Thursdays are thrilling,
Fridays are fabulous,
Saturdays are supreme,
Sundays are spectacular,
Each day is different,
And every day's new.

Sophie Russell (11)
Cirencester Kingshill School, Cirencester

The Streets Of Today

The streets of today, what do you see?
Do you like what you see? Can you change it?
Graffiti on the walls,
Pollution-filled air,
Ruined environment,
Yobs swearing and making no sense,
Neighbours arguing,
And littered streets.
Can we change it too?
The streets of tomorrow,
Clean and tidy,
Sweet fragrant air,
People walking to work
And overflowing dustbins.
We want this, can we get it?
Is it possible? You answer the question,
You make the decision, you make it happen.

Zoe Hollebon (12)
Cirencester Kingshill School, Cirencester

Alone . . .

Somewhere yet nowhere,
Cold and alone.

Painless yet painful,
Without any home.

Ghostly, invisible
Dirty and cramped.

Colourless and hungry
Floor's hard and damp.

Wishing and hoping
Hollow and unfair.

Lightless and lifeless.
Alone, alone.

Jess Stockford (13)
Cirencester Kingshill School, Cirencester

The Homeless Man

Like a ghost he drifts, from doorway to doorway,
Solitary and hollow, haunting the streets,
Fruitlessly seeking the warmth of the shadows,
Scurrying for cover as the skies start to weep.
Sheltering in an alleyway, he's found a dirty step
Here he shall stay to rest his head
The dangers of the night he is trying to forget,
Lying amongst the litter in his concrete bed.

His eyes are constantly searching,
Peering, through the blackest night,
The darkness is like a heavy shroud, enveloping his body.
Wide awake he ponders his plight,
He moans as the icy wind bruises his bones
And he is numbed within,
Disconnected footsteps pound the pavement,
Silence
And he is alone again.

Now he's disturbed from a fitful slumber
As day breaks and -
The weak winter sunlight
Illuminates a world all shades of grey.
Hopeless and hungry, penniless, in pain.
His soul is empty, eyes glazed,
He rises to resume his mantra -
Always asking; 'Got any change?'

Emma Benton (13)
Cirencester Kingshill School, Cirencester

All About Me

My name is Jade, I'm a really cool kid.
I live with my family and I have a cat called Sid.
I have lots of friends and I like to play.
I like to laze around on Saturday.

Jade Smith (13)
Cirencester Kingshill School, Cirencester

Heartbreaker

The day he asked me I was thrilled,
The day he dumped me I was killed.

The day he kissed me I thought it was a dream,
The day he told me I wanted to scream.

The day he hugged me I was glad,
The day he laughed at me I was mad.

The day he held my hand it was like I could forget,
The day he walked away I was so upset.

The day he came I felt so strong,
The day he left I felt so wrong.

At first I was happy,
Then I was sad,
In the end I was really mad.

He broke my heart into thousands of pieces,
I thought it would last,
But no,
It went away so fast . . .

Hannah Dawkins (13)
Cirencester Kingshill School, Cirencester

All I Want Is . . .

Feeling depressed, every day
The cold, hard concrete where I lay
All I want is a bite to eat.

Mmm fish and chips, or even a plate of veg and meat
I can taste them in my mouth
I know it can't be any good for my health
But all I want is a bite to eat.

Any change please is what I say
No sorry just get out my way
But all I want is a bite to eat.

Emma Lambert (14)
Cirencester Kingshill School, Cirencester

Miss You

I miss you.
Without you it hasn't been the same.
I almost cry when I hear your name.
Even though you're gone we're still a team.
Nobody knows what you mean to me.
You always showed love.
Your face like doves
You never left me alone because you care for me.
Why couldn't God leave us be.
I suppose you were needed up in the blue.
I really miss you.
Cancer got the best.
But it couldn't get the rest.
Memories give me what I need.
The strength to believe.
I pray I go to Heaven to see you again - Amen.
I miss you Grandma.

Joseph Watkins (13)
Cirencester Kingshill School, Cirencester

Time To Leave

As the relentless icy concrete
Takes its toll on my body
I feel invisible
And I go to haunt a doorway for the night.

As I stand and ask, 'Spare some change mate?'
It's futile
I can't even bring myself to smile
Who cares about an unloved dosser making this town look bad
I never even got a chance to see my dad.

They say it's your own fault making yourself like this,
I spend a lot of time thinking of what I miss
Here comes those pigs again
I guess I had better go then.

James Freeman (13)
Cirencester Kingshill School, Cirencester

The City

The city was deadly silent
The only occupants willing to show their faces were the birds
                                                    and the rats

And even they were cautious
Silent, deadly, haunted
The graffiti of a thousand ages lined upon every wall
Silent, deadly, haunted
The smoke from every block like fog never rising
Silent, deadly, haunted
The distant sirens breaking the evil silence, a wolf howling
                                                    in the night,
Silent, deadly, haunted
The barbed wire blocking off this place from the world of civilisation
Silent, deadly, haunted
Silent, deadly, haunted
Silent, deadly, haunted . . . gone.

Matt Perry (13)
Cirencester Kingshill School, Cirencester

Rubbish Arsenal

I hate you Arsenal I do!
I just want to flush you down the loo
I hate you Arsenal I do!
Arsenal you're so rubbish and poo!

Your manager is as bright as a bench
All he does is buy the French
The whole team is full of scum
So get your head out of your . . . ahem

You beat Real Madrid 1-0 by luck,
But on that night Real Madrid did suck
Madrid are still the best with Becks on our side
Ronaldo can't get in the team because he's too wide.

Tom Gardiner (12)
Cirencester Kingshill School, Cirencester

Homeless Poem

I feel bad,
Very very sad.

I need a home,
Where I'm not alone,
A family to see,
But I know it is never going to be.

I'm feeling freezing,
My feet are seizing,
Up.

Looking for a job is pointless,
They have made me hopeless.

I'm feeling all hollow,
Please do not follow.

I am a nervous wreck,
Do not reject.

I sleep on the hard,
I get so many bruises I'm scarred.

The voices I hear,
As people cheer,
They come from a beer,
I sit here in fear.

Loren Cowling (13)
Cirencester Kingshill School, Cirencester

The City

As I walk along the rundown old road,
I see shops as empty as a pie without filling,
There are gangs gathering like moths to the flame
And cars abandoned like unwanted pets.
The buildings crumbling like the lost city of Atlantis.
I come to an end, an end that's as dark as a blackout,
But is it the end?

Oliver Shurmer (13)
Cirencester Kingshill School, Cirencester

The City

The city was dull and gloomy,
Like a blanket of dark mist,
The high-sky flats towering over,
Like stacks of black burnt toast.

The streets were like lots of dark tunnels,
Leading further and further into the city,
With a hot, clammy wind,
Just like a hairdryer on full blast.

The sidewalks covered in glass,
As sharp as a butcher's knife.
Graffiti covering the walls,
Like a toddler's first painting.

I wandered the lonely city,
Like a lost ghost,
Trying to find my spirit again.

Sophie Benson (13)
Cirencester Kingshill School, Cirencester

The City

Barbed wire waiting to strike
Like a horrific medieval knight
Crumbling flats deserted and destroyed
Murderous locals angry and annoyed.

Abandoned and alight
A truly revolting sight
Looted shops
Too horrendous for cops,

Sharp shattered glass
Everywhere you pass
You can't feel safe along the street
Or otherwise you're dead meat!

Matt Berry (14)
Cirencester Kingshill School, Cirencester

Poem For Homeless People

I'm walking on down the cold, hard street,
And I see all these dossers looking utterly beat.
And I think, maybe, just maybe they're not all winos
Half dead from the drink -
No - no, don't think that, conform, be normal, go along with
What you're told you must think.
They're drunk, dossers, deranged and dying,
They have no life, no personality, no hope -
No hope? What does it feel like to have no hope?
No direction in life - broken dreams.
Cramped into a mould that doesn't quite fit.
An outcast - exiled, derelict and forgotten.
Listening
Listening,
Listening to the beat of feet on the street.
Listening,
Listening,
Listening to the jingle of unwanted change bouncing in pockets . . .
Why don't they stop? Why don't they have some empathy?
To be invisible, to be a non-person -
What does it feel like?

Jenny Hayhurst (13)
Cirencester Kingshill School, Cirencester

Christmas

C hristmas presents being opened everywhere
H appy faces across the world
R ipping presents open
I nside more decorations going up
S anta came and left presents.
T he tree is looking great, shining bright
M erry Christmas everyone
A ll the presents I wanted
S melling the dinner nearly done.

Megan Tipper (12)
Cirencester Kingshill School, Cirencester

Awaiting For The Gates

As I wandered down the lonely city,
I passed the doorway to Hell,
Dark and daunting,
Like it had no right or place to be there.

When I crept away from the dangerous, deadly door,
The clouds took up my thoughts,
Dull and heavy,
Like a pile of wet clothes,
Just brought out from the washing machine.

Whilst I walked along the silent but busy streets,
I noticed the old, tall crumbling flats,
Reminding me of an old cake
Dying to be eaten.

I saw the gates open to Heaven,
As I approached the destination I had been awaiting for,
I felt the sweat off my back soaking into my top,
It was just like the flood back in '89,
I felt so lost.

Beth Gray (13)
Cirencester Kingshill School, Cirencester

The Farm

My name is Clover
I live on the white cliffs of Dover
I have a dog, she rounds up sheep
But all they do is bleat and bleat
And in the barn I have a cow
Her name is Daisy
And she likes to sleep when it's hazy.

In the sty there are some pigs
And one of their names is Little Miss Brigs
She spies on the man right next door
He's the pig she does adore.

Charley Yates (12)
Cirencester Kingshill School, Cirencester

Nothing

Nothing
I'm invisible
Stalking the streets
Shadows, darkness.

Sitting
The cruel pavement beneath me
Hard, senseless
Stone cold.

Longing for food
Hungry, starving
But there's no chance
None.

I beg
I hope
But still
Nothing.

Ted Sales (13)
Cirencester Kingshill School, Cirencester

The Seaside

The sand was golden like the sun.
Children sat clutching their ice cream
Like swans protecting their young.
The seagulls swarm the children like a lion
For its meat.
The sea glistens like diamonds as it
Swallowed up all the sandcastles that had took the
Whole day to make.
As the sun started to go down the people started to go,
As I walked the lonely beach
I thought about how the whole beach had changed
And by tomorrow the whole system will start all over again.

Natasha Taylor (14)
Cirencester Kingshill School, Cirencester

My Cat

The furry friend,
Cute and cool
That is my cat.

Miaowing, howling,
Sorry sounding
But cute and cuddly
My cat's like that.

A playing, peering,
Mewing, prowling thing
That is my cat she likes that.

Sleeping and creeping
My cat she really likes that.

My cat, my cat,
What will we do
With that cat?

Georgina Shorter (13)
Cirencester Kingshill School, Cirencester

Friends

Standing by,
All the way.
Have to help you through your day.

Holding you up
When you are weak,
Helping you find what it is you seek.

Catching your tears,
When you cry
Pulling you through when the tide is high.

Just being there,
Through thick and thin,
All just to say, you are my friend.

Charlie Walker (12)
Cirencester Kingshill School, Cirencester

Why? Who? What? When? How?

Why can't pigs fly?
Why is the sky blue?
Why do mirrors crack?
And what's a gnu?

Why do dogs woof?
Why do cats purr?
Why do lions roar?
Why do hamsters have fur?

What noise does a rabbit make?
What sound does a slug shout?
Why do frogs go splat?
And what are fish all about?

Why can't whales walk?
Why does a man have a 'wife'?
Why can't we all sing?
And what's the meaning of life?

Are you feeling silly?
Do you smell like spam?
Are you feeling stupid?
I know I am!

Abby Wharton (13)
Cirencester Kingshill School, Cirencester

A Poem Of Poems

P oems are sometimes people's life stories
O thers are just snippets of their imagination
E ven some have metaphors
M any of them rhyme
S ome even use similies

R egularly they have alliteration
O thers often use fun memories
C hildhood is a very good topic to do a poem on
K eep those rules in mind and you will make a great poet.

Georgina Gale (13)
Cirencester Kingshill School, Cirencester

She's My Dog!

Annie's terror
Annie's mad
Annie's naughty
Annie's bad!

She chews your feet
And moans at night
She steals your socks
And hurts when she bites.

When she's naughty
She runs upstairs
And when you catch her
You're covered in hairs.

She drives me crazy
She drives me mad
But when she cries
I feel guilty and sad!

When she's good
We get peace and quiet
But when she's loud
We start a *riot!*

Mollie Shute (12)
Cirencester Kingshill School, Cirencester

Rain

I'm standing here in the rain
Drip-drop! Splash!
Rain dripping on my head.
Drip-drop! Splash!
Time is ticking
Drip-drop! Splash!
The sun is starting to break through.
Drip-drop!
I'm standing here in the sun.
Bright! Shimmer! Shine!

Laura Outram (12)
Cirencester Kingshill School, Cirencester

Life Of An Army Man

My old man is in the army
He owns a really big gun
When he went to Afghanistan
He started shooting everyone.

His gun is a rifle
It is really big
He hasn't no hair
So he has to wear a wig.

His job is very dangerous
In the army life
Especially in Iraq
Where he was threatened with a knife.

My old man is a warrant officer
That is a high rank
It is so high
That he gets to drive a tank.

The reason he is in the army
Because he is really strong
He has got really big muscles
His nickname is King Kong.

Senegal and the Falkland Islands
My old man those places he has been
Kenya and Belgium
Those places to go he is very keen.

Johnathon Keary (12)
Cirencester Kingshill School, Cirencester

The City

Like cars crammed in on the motorway,
The city was busy,
There was twisted and rusty barbed wire,
Tangled around and around the city walls.

The church, a cathedral stood above the rest,
It was grand,
And impressive,
Like a proud poodle parading at Crufts.

The shops were rundown and dirty,
The centre was covered with litter, unclean and disgusting, like a
Rainbow
With mud trampled all over.

On the walls there was graffiti,
Rude,
It had been there for years, like
The tramps had been,
The tramps, who had flies circling their head,
As if they were in a Formula 1 race.

Behind all of the junk and dirt came the rest of the city,
Offices, apartments and posh restaurants,
The new area at the suburbs of town, celebrities come and leave,
The trees whistle in the wind
Again the edge of the city thinks, all-awaiting, all prepared,
The offices may be amazing,
But as the monster clock strikes twelve,
It will change.

Chris Hasking (14)
Cirencester Kingshill School, Cirencester

Favourite Things

F avourite things
A re something special
V ery important to you
O h and don't let me forget
U can have them too
R eally good
I n their own way
T hey can be big or small
E ven something tall

T o everyone
H ave someone
I n their life
N ot a nasty thing, someone
G ood and
S pecial.

Harriet Fox (12)
Cirencester Kingshill School, Cirencester

My Poem

The city was calm,
The sun was shining bright,
Barbed wire everywhere rusted and blood
Tipped like a vampire's teeth.
Crumbling flats sat decayed and grey,
Old smelly rubbish hid like a tramp,
In the dull grey doorway.
The shops closed down and covered
In obscene graffiti.
Lorries overturned and abandoned.
In amongst it all a church stood proud and
Tall, all grand like a poodle
At Crufts. Like a winner in amongst the
Losers.

Matt Reynolds (13)
Cirencester Kingshill School, Cirencester

Things I Could Do

The world's so big,
So many things to do before I die.
But if I could I would,
Learn to drive,
Race like the Stig.
Get sick on a roller coaster.
Freefall out of the Concorde
Deep-sea dive.

Swim with dolphins,
Hold onto sharks' fins.
Climb the Swiss Alps,
Meet the Celts.
Walk the wall of China,
Don't know what could be finer.
Come face to face with the terracotta army,
Climb Uluru,
The weather could be balmy.

Of all the things I could do before I die,
These are a select few.

Nick Mellor (12)
Cirencester Kingshill School, Cirencester

Trapped

What's up there above the sky?
Why does everyone have to die?

Watching all the fields go by
What's it like to fly up high?

While others are just playing darts
I'm trapped here in the dark.

I'm sitting in this lousy place,
Thinking what's out there in space.

Seeing everyone's happy face
I'm stuck here in this dark, cramped place.

Sebastian Johnson (13)
Cirencester Kingshill School, Cirencester

Tomato Ketchup

How I love my ketchup
I have it with everything
Like chocolate, crisps, bananas and chips
All my friends think I'm ming
My friends think I'm disgusting
But I just say it's nice
And if they ever get the chance
They should try it with some rice.

Last night we had a sleepover
I thought it was really great
Apart from when my friend teased me
For having too much ketchup on my plate
I said to my friends to try it
And it really wasn't that bad
But when one of them tried it and puked
I felt really sad.

Tom Sutton (13)
Cirencester Kingshill School, Cirencester

Life In The City

I once knew this old town
But now, there are
Old men on the ground.
They live behind the fence of the park
Like old dustbins.
The fence is
Like a huge army with long spears to
Protect them.
The school is
Rundown with broken windows and with graffiti,
As rude as a streaker running across
The pitch of a football game.
The school used to be full of children
And teachers but now they've given up
And kids have smashed it up like bombs.

Finlay Rochfort (13)
Cirencester Kingshill School, Cirencester

The City

As I dawdled through the city
I noticed its warmth
Like the sun on a hot summer's day
The cathedral stood visible from anywhere
Tall and important
Like the Queen on her throne.

The stunning, Victorian houses sat
Open and welcoming
Like a playhouse in a nursery.

The busy, bustling shops
Were like Waitrose before Christmas.

The preschool children walked
Obediently at their mother's side
Smiling politely at passers-by.

The expensive cars
Showed off revving their engines
Like boy racers on the racetracks.

Alice Christopher (13)
Cirencester Kingshill School, Cirencester

Autumn!

I love it when it's autumn,
When the leaves fall to the ground.
They're as light as small feathers,
They fall without a sound.

The leaves get swept to huge piles,
They get really, really high.
And when you go and jump in them,
It makes the old people sigh!

It's the time of year,
That the rugby season begins.
I go and watch the matches,
Hoping that Gloucester wins!

Harriet Vickery (12)
Cirencester Kingshill School, Cirencester

The City

The city was bustling.
Like the Eiffel Tower watching
Over Paris, tall and dominant
Was the tree.
Rubbish unwanted like
The runt of the litter of pigs.
Like a TV the traffic lights
Flashing and over-used.
Dark and mischievous like
The Grim Reaper was the alley.
The paths like a tightrope walk
Were narrow.
Like a train leaving a station bulky
And noise was the lorries.
Like a wasp's nest the shops
Were busy.
Offices were active like an ant
Digging a tunnel.
Barbed wire was like a rhino's horn,
Sharp and deadly,
That is how I see the city.

Craig Aylett (13)
Cirencester Kingshill School, Cirencester

Autumn Days

A utumn days are the best
U ngrateful squirrels steal the birds' food
T he grass is always moist with dew
U nder the trees lies all of its leaves
M orning is rising, all the birds are singing
N ow the wind is getting a lot stronger.

D ays are sunny but are mainly cold
A ll the insects are beginning to die
Y ellow, orange leaves start to fall
S quirrels are about to hibernate.

Ben Chapman (13)
Cirencester Kingshill School, Cirencester

I Was

The red car swerved around the corner,
The man chucked me in it,
I was scared.

The wind was on my face like a shot
I was freezing cold sat by the car,
I was afraid.

The grass was all around me
Swaying to and fro,
I was relaxed.

I ended up at a house
He dragged me in,
I was crying.

I heard a siren outside,
The police burst in,
I was happy.

The sound of happiness hugged me tight
The feel of a bed felt soothing,
I was safe.

Kirstie Jarvis (13)
Cirencester Kingshill School, Cirencester

Star

I am a star
50,000 light years away
A burning ball of gas
Floating in the universe
Things from planet Earth staring up at us
We are just stars, why do they stare up
In amazement and awe?
Comets shine bright
Tails millions of miles long
In the ray of the sun
In Earth's twilight.

Rachel Ody (13)
Cirencester Kingshill School, Cirencester

The City

I walk along the lonely road
Now silent, now pierced by
Screeching sirens.
Above, barbed wire looming
On top of high walls, coiled,
Waiting to swoop down and
Attack.
Below me as I walk the
Pavement cracked and uneven,
Piles of rubbish too disgusting
To look at, too huge to ignore.
Flats on either side,
Dominating the skyline,
Tall and bare, huddling
Together to block out
The sunlight.
Squalid offices,
Mere skeletons of their
Former glory, filled with people
Scurrying in and out,
Like rats carrying on with
Their mundane lives, just
Waiting to die.
On the sidewalk cars are
Desolate, hardly able to stand,
Left only with a rusty
Frame to shield it from
The harsh winter wind.
Shops, closed and rundown,
Morbid reminders
Of the hopes lost to the
Ravages of time.
The people, eyes like
Hungry dogs
Desperate for food,
Warmth and love.

Zoe Shaw (13)
Cirencester Kingshill School, Cirencester

My Dad's Socks

My dad's socks are smelly
Because they're always in his wellies,
He never changes them
Because they're his favourite socks.

My dad's socks are holey
Because he says they're holy,
He never gets a new pair
Because they're his best socks.

My dad's socks are odd
On them they've got policemen plod,
He doesn't say they're old
Because they're his first pair of socks.

However my dad's socks are the best
Because birds could make a nest,
He says his feet are the only thing in his socks
Because they're his *only* socks!

George Ford (12)
Cirencester Kingshill School, Cirencester

The Ruined City

The city with the flats, the huge grey giants
And its rusted barbed wire like an evil smile
And its broken church like a discarded child's doll.
In the wreck of a city with its burnt out buildings and the graffiti,
The horrible graffiti and broken lorries
And rotting dead animals in the street.
Elsewhere amongst the broken street lights
And the discarded rubbish,
As the wind howled through the streets
Moving the broken glass that litters all the streets.
There was an old school before the change
Now all that lives there are tramps
And they listen to the giant clock in the broken clock tower.

Alex Martin (13)
Cirencester Kingshill School, Cirencester

Rabbits Out And About

As I watch you eating your carrot,
I realise that I didn't much want a parrot.
I didn't know that I had a habit
Of getting loads of rabbits.
But when I put you in your run,
I see you having fun,
Then a bee flies by,
And when I look up at the sky,
I realise that,
You really don't like rats.
Now it's getting late,
Unlucky mate!
Time to go away
Ready for another day.

Jade Mathieson (12)
Cirencester Kingshill School, Cirencester

Smurfs And Life

Little blue bodies and
Little white hats.

Living in mushrooms
Running through forests.

Then kersplatt
Cancelled, gone.

After years of entertainment,
Fun and song.

They are the Smurfs.

How very much like life.

James Preston (12)
Cirencester Kingshill School, Cirencester

The Deadly Dragon

In the lonely-hearted forest
Is a dragon named Flame,
Though you'd probably wonder why that's his so-called name.

He hunts and hunts
'Til he finds some fleshy food,
But he only comes out most nights when he's in the mood.

On his rough, delicate forehead
Reads an ancient Japanese sign,
It says: what is all yours can also be mine.

He creeps through the dark, damp dungeons,
He flies through the rusty old doors
And crumbles on the hard stony floors.

You would probably think in that brain of yours
What a weird little dragon,
That is what you are gonna imagine.

His wings stretch out so wide
That you could use them as a barrier wall,
He could go so high and so small.

Everyone who sees this gigantic savage
Will run so fast that their legs will break
And hopefully this won't be their only mistake,
'Cause tonight the monster will sleep and eat
And make the humans his deadly meat.

So sleep well tonight,
'Cause you might get a very big fright,
When the dragon named Flame comes to rip off a bite,
Oh, I do hope you sleep well tonight.

Emma Lawrence (12)
Cirencester Kingshill School, Cirencester

Teaching!

I don't know what I'm doing.
I don't know what to do.
I'm looking out the window,
Not looking at you.

You finally see me
Just about to shout
But in comes a teacher
Just looking, looking short and stout.

She looks at me calmly
And says, 'Get on with your work'
Then the teacher said
'Don't you dare smirk.'

I hate school
I do, I do, I do
I know I'll hide
I'll stay in the loo.
'But you have to go to school'
My husband said
'You have to go
You're the Head.'

Charles Buse (12)
Cirencester Kingshill School, Cirencester

The Bad Boy At School

The bad boy is back;
Terrorising people again,
He smashed my MP3 Player,
I hate him like everyone else.

The bad boy is here,
Swearing at teachers again,
He snapped my brand new pencil,
I hate him even more.

The bad boy is fiendish,
Beating up toddlers again,
He cooked poor Timmy's puppy in a frying pan,
Now Timmy hates him too.

The bad boy has gone,
Not beating, smashing or snapping,
I gave him a taste of his own medicine,
Just like everyone else.

But now he has gone,
Said that I bullied him,
So I'm sitting in detention,
I'm just as bad as him.

Max Clayton (12)
Cirencester Kingshill School, Cirencester

Black And White

I'm at home on my own
Looking at photos.
They are all black and white,
But still,
I like them all.
One question remains in my head,
Why are people racist?
Black or white, or slightly tanned,
We're all born in the same way,
No one should be insulted,
And still,
One question remains in my head,
Why are people racist?

Mitch Potts (12)
Cirencester Kingshill School, Cirencester

Life!

Life is a gift
You can't wish for things,
You can't make things happen,
You have limited time on this Earth,
So use it well,
Do what you want,
Not what others want.
Don't look back on the past,
Look to the future.
It's your life,
Live it to the full.
And live!

Joanne Alderman (12)
Cirencester Kingshill School, Cirencester

Mischievous Martin And His Time Machine

Just imagine going back in time
Then I wouldn't have to write this rhyme
I could go back in history
Change everything just for me.

All schools demolished
All rules abolished.

British bulldog reinstated,
All teachers forever sedated.

But if I did sedate the teachers,
Yes sleepify all the preachers!
We would be so dumb,
That we wouldn't know the one plus one sum.

Luke Oosthuizen (12)
Cirencester Kingshill School, Cirencester

Me The Dolphin

I am a dolphin. I live in the sea.
I meet a friend, they're kind to me.

I jump through the waves and dance with the sand.
While listening to an ocean band.

I dive here and I dive there
Over the waves without a care.

Happily I talk and play
In the water every day.

I'm so beautiful and smart,
Surely a wonderful work of art.

Emma Legg (12)
Cirencester Kingshill School, Cirencester

Being A Goat

I am a goat,
I live on a boat.
One day the captain said,
I should have a cuddly, comfy bed.

We landed on a beautiful inhabited island,
The land was named the Highlands.
I met a beautiful goat there,
It had long, shiny white hair.

She is called Dove,
She is my true love.
I followed her to the lake,
Where we felt the ground quake.

We ran for cover,
Where we cuddled each other.
We soon found,
That it was the buffalos running around.

We grazed in the meadow,
Then watched our children grow
We were happy together,
So I stayed there forever.

Rebecca Hicks (12)
Cirencester Kingshill School, Cirencester

Battlefield

I'm in a trench,
The stench of battle wafts along the line.
Putrid, vile, bullets flying.
Malice encrusts my mind.
Shots boom, rain pelting . . . pelting . . . pelting.
You hear the snarl of death rise up.
Sight becomes hazy, shouts turn to nothingness.
Bland as a machine.
Fire blazes, I tremble and stoop,
Plummet down into the foetus of the battlefield.
I hear no more pain decrepit.

I wade slushing through the nearly impregnable golden corn,
I see the gates that await my soul.
Frittilaries flash in outrageous bursts,
Dragonflies loom ahead, resilient in gloom's path.
I hear the joyous laughter of my child,
Acquiescence seeps my eyes,
Like fire to matchwood, I crisply reawaken.
The gates surge upwards, tower afore,
Rejoice, my heart succumbs to all the intensity of eternity.

Memor-oris icis, remember them.

James O'Leary (12)
Cirencester Kingshill School, Cirencester

Runaway Horse

As I jump upon the leather saddle and
Grab hold of the well-worn reins
My horse and I knew that we were off.
Galloping through fields; jumping gates,
Chasing birds and rabbits.
The power of the horse's legs after every stride
Was making me want to go faster and faster,
Over miles and miles.
It felt like all of my problems were being blown away
In the wind and that nothing could stop me.
The sweat pouring off the neck and shoulders of the large animal,
Its eyes filled with fire and strength,
Its hooves brushing the grass, and the veins and muscles showing
on its skin.
Passing through woods and lakes, farms and tracks,
Not knowing where I was leading my horse, but knowing for sure
The wind was leading us to a place where there were fields and forests
To race through, lakes and ponds to splash about in
And somewhere my horse and I could be happy and free together . . .
Forever!

Rosie Mizon (12)
Cirencester Kingshill School, Cirencester

The Window

There was a window
In the mist,
I looked to my right,
I looked to my left.
There was a girl,
Oh it was me,
My reflection looking back at me.
When it is late at night
The stars are out
They shine so bright.

Rayner Killingback (11)
Cirencester Kingshill School, Cirencester

The City

The city bustled with traffic and people making their way to work.

Like a lemur's tail curled around a tree
The barbed wire fencing was twisted and starting to rust around
The industrial work grounds.

The noise of cars speeding round the city centre sounded as if
They were wild lions looking after their territory.

The church like a giraffe walking the plains was high up and proud,
As it looked over the city's people, watching them come and go
In the foggy daylight.

As if they were clouds on a sunny day, the grey stained flats
Peered out over the busy narrow roads.

Similar to African ant hills, the piles of rubbish
Spread out across the quiet but mysterious back paths.

The dingy shop was boarded up as if it was an old moth-eaten chair
Covered by a sheet.

Like a kid crying out for attention the dribbled forgotten graffiti
                                        lay caked
On the flaking walls and bus stops.

Similar to a single rose the lorry lay abandoned
On the roadside.

The city bustled with traffic and people making their way to work.

Emma Byrnes (13)
Cirencester Kingshill School, Cirencester

Jimmy And The Witch

Here's a story - strange but true
About a boy called Jim,
Whose mum and dad went out one night
And left a witch with him.

She said she was a sitter
And good with children too,
But all she really wanted was
To make Jim into stew!

I guess you couldn't blame her
He was an awful brat,
She waved her magic wand at Jim
And changed him to a rat.

She chased him round the kitchen
He hid inside the sink,
She turned him to a smelly skunk
That caused a horrid stink!

Jim made a break for freedom
And ran out of the door,
But he couldn't get away
And Jimmy is no more.

Coral Stratford-Smith (12)
Cirencester Kingshill School, Cirencester

Forget Snooker

He's on for the blue, now to the pink,
Just the black left, he's won the frame!

Watching a break of 148
But what do we care? It's just too late
To be thinking about a stupid cue ball,
Hitting the colours, in the pockets they fall.

He's on for the blue, now to the pink,
Just the black left, he's won the frame!

Why can't they cut to MOTD 2
Instead of seeing Shaun Murphy chalk up his cue?
Why don't they let us be
And put on something we want to see?

He's on for the blue, now to the pink,
Just the black left, he's won the frame!

I can't watch this anymore, it's all I can take!
Up and down go the balls like sweeping up leaves with a rake.
Please put the snooker on BBCi
Do it now, before I die!

He's on for the blue, now to the pink,
Just the black left, he's won the game!

James Eynon (13)
Culverhay School, Bath

Boom! Boom! Boom!

Boom! Boom! Boom!
Blasts the stereo loud
You could hear this music
If you were up in the clouds.

Speakers being sucked in
And then being blown out
The fish swim away
All following the trout!

Mum sitting downstairs
Can't hear herself think
And Dad in the shower
Can't tell if he stinks!

Speakers being sucked in
And then being blown out
The fish swim away
All following the trout!

Seagulls turn back
As the sound waves repel
A man knocks on the door
And asks 'What the hell . . .

. . . is going on here
in this house full of noise?
My granddaughter next door
Is trying to play with her toys!

But she can't concentrate
Cos this music's too loud
You could hear this music
If you were up in the clouds!'

Joe Payne (14)
Culverhay School, Bath

Concorde

There it goes, flying through the air,
Gliding its carbon fibre wings
The pointy nose, with people below stare,
The enjoyment this graceful beauty brings.

The BA flag shines bright soaring through the sky,
Flying faster than sound, shaking the ground
The brutal force of the engine makes young kids cry,
Until one day she lost the sound.

There it goes, flying through the air,
Gliding its carbon fibre wings
The pointy nose with people below stare,
The enjoyment this graceful beauty brings.

In Paris one day her engine decided to go,
Although it wasn't her fault
She was put down in service which spoilt the airline's flow,
Because of a stupid runaway runway battery with a high volt.

There it goes, flying through the air,
Gliding its carbon fibred wings
The pointy nose, with people below stare,
The enjoyment this graceful beauty brings.

She is now on a stand in Filton Bristol,
Rusting away which should be stopped
She should be remade of diamond and crystal,
She will be remembered not forgot.

There it went, flying through the air,
Gliding her carbon fibre wings
The pointy nose with people below stared,
The enjoyment this graceful beauty brang!

Liam Hutchison (14)
Culverhay School, Bath

My Family

Irritated, moody, red-faced grin,
Stony-faced, stressed, stropping and grim,
Agitated, furious, angry and mad,
That's my grumpy old grandad.
He is always very sad.

Creepy and cunning, curious and quiet,
Twinkle-toed and skinny, always on a diet,
Hesitant, inquisitive, nosey and sly,
That's my annoying sister,
She always cries.

Almighty and athletic, confident and strong,
Always powerful, persistent and healthy,
He says he is never wrong,
Nice and giving, never bad,
He is the best and that's my dad.

Eccentric, energetic, entertaining and fun,
Always working hard,
That's my mum.

Evil, spiteful, not very nice,
Mean and horrible, always starting fights,
Never shuts up, that's my brother,
Always beating me up, causing me bother.

But then again life is hard for every living being,
We all get upset once in a while,
We are worse than babies teething.

Luke Taylor (14)
Culverhay School, Bath

Weather And Places Spoken In Autumn

The sun-soaked days are now bygone
With the windy willow truly felled.

The gas turned on,
The fires sparked,
Mother Nature's way leaves an evil path.

The Yorkshire Dales covered in frost,
With the gas man's list counting the cost.

There'll be no more revels,
On the Somerset levels,
Unless we heed the warning
Of global warming.

The Dawlish sea wall protecting the trains,
Soon washed away by waves and rains.

Hand-freezing snow in late December,
Gives us good old memories forever and ever.

The Lancashire estates with smoke from their chimneys,
A scene so different from the West Indies.

The thundery rain on Thursday mornings,
Make half-term days unbelievably boring.

So from no question,
I've made an answer
That the weather's much bleaker when spoken in autumn.

Steven Toogood (13)
Culverhay School, Bath

The Dead Have Voices Too . . .

Take a little trip through the plains of the dead
A place where the nightmares run free and wild
The land of no colour, of monotone grey
Take a look around you - do you like what you see?
Is this really where you want to be?

And always remember - the dead have voices too.

Take a little trip down the path of the past
A place where mistakes run free and wild
The land of failure, of direst cruelty,
Take a look around you - do you like what you see?
Is this really where you want to be?

And always remember - failure is a portal, good or bad.

Take a little trip through the halls of learning
A place where words run free and wild
The land of no action, where they cling to the past
Take a look around you - do you like what you see?
Is this really where you want to be?

And always remember - rules are not rules until they're broken.

Take a little trip to the corner of the world
A place where the lost ones run free and wild
The land of no hope, where they walk on the edge
Take a look around you - do you like what you see?
Is this really where you want to be?

And always remember - soon they will be gone . . .

. . . But the dead have voices too . . .

Rebecca Whalley (14)
Downend School, Bristol

Autumn

The wind is howling like a scared dog,
The brownie, yellow leaves are falling from the blue sky,
The children are playing under the bare trees,
The animals are collecting food for the cold winter.

There's grey, dark clouds forming,
Fires burning,
Children singing like birds would sing on a spring morning.

The rain is falling like a child crying,
The damp leaves are going all soggy and mushy,
Adults and children are huddled under umbrellas,
Waiting in the cold damp morning,
Waiting for the school bell to ring.

I can hear thudding on the roof of my warm house,
I cuddle into my warm and cosy bed,
The rain stopped thudding suddenly.

I tried to spot the rabbits but there are none to be seen,
All I can see is the warm sun shining on the muddy grass,
All the lovely smelling flowers have gone,
All there is is mud where the green grass should be growing.
Oh how I love the autumn.

Sophie Chapman
Downend School, Bristol

Autumn Poem

'Crunch, crunch'
The leaves lying dead,
Summer has gone, go early to bed.
The days get darker,
So are the leaves,
To crunchy brown, from juicy green.
Really cold mornings,
Don't want to wake up,
Sleeping through the alarm, is a habit we have got.
Lonely lying leaves asleep cold breezes,
No sound in the mornings, except loud sneezes.
Foggy mornings,
Misty roads,
The wind moves the leaves to and fro.
Oh the rain that we fear,
On our cheeks look like tears,
Goodbye autumn it's time to leave, so the trees regain
Their leaves.

Lauren Woodman (13)
Downend School, Bristol

Through The Eyes Of . . . A Bird

The Earth does not serve trouble for me,
As I can leave it far behind,
When I'm soaring high, over land and sea,
With others of my kind.

And I do behold such bliss,
When gliding over town,
The people stare, unwilling to miss,
My method of getting around.

And on realising humans' bizarre creations,
To escape gravity's strain,
We are filled with the realisation,
That it is our flight they wish to gain.

Eleanor Child (12)
Hayesfield School, Bath

It's A Dog's Life

My owner really loved me,
But I think he was quite old
And then one day, he went away,
And I was shut out in the cold.

I was crammed into a wire cage
And treated like a pig.
Then after what seems a lifetime in there,
I grew to be quite big.

They moved me to a bigger hutch,
With more space so I could walk,
There were also other dogs in there
That were too sad to talk.

'Hello,' I'd cry, 'How are you?' I'd say
But I never got any reply
For the dogs that were in this dogs' home
Looked almost ready to die.

When at last a small girl looked at me,
'He's cute!' I heard her say!
'I could brush up his fur and I would love him lots!
Please let me buy him today!'

When I got my new home I barked for joy
Then I heard a scream and barked faster
Because of all my vicious barking,
I had scared away my master.

I managed to find her on her bed,
I tried to say 'I love you'
And then my whole world lifted around me
She said, 'I love you too!'

Claire Berrisford (12)
Hayesfield School, Bath

War

Clothed in stale sweat,
We stood there like scarecrows.
Standing only because of the rotting poles of some futile hope,
That was steadily being crushed by the rippings of Man.
Dead and mud marooning us,
Twisted bodies holding inside,
Then a single wish to die.
Then there came the shout -

'Gas. East side. Hurry!'
It came creeping across,
Searching with strangling tendrils,
I fumbled,
It entwined me,
I was drowning,
Drowning on land,
It took me,
I wanted to die,
To stop,
To finish,
I did.

Ruth Byfield (12)
Hayesfield School, Bath

A Different World

Dolphins diving in a salty world
Grey sleek smoothness, swishing,
Coloured coral swaying,
A whirl of colours playing.

A salty rippling pallet,
Mixing blue and green,
A turquoise heaven sparkling
The sunlight of a different world, it seems.

Annie Walker-Trafford (12)
Hayesfield School, Bath

Shoes

Shoes glorious shoes,
Three high heels and slippers,
What more could you need,
Topshop and Tammies,
Etam and Asda,
Select and Clarks
Oh shoes wonderful shoes,
Magical shoes,
Glorious shoes.

Flicking through the catalogue,
Wishing I could get some
One moment of knowing that
Full grown feeling.
Oh shoes wonderful shoes,
Magical shoes,
Glorious shoes.

Chelsea Buchan (12)
Hayesfield School, Bath

Turn Back Time

I wish I could turn back time
So many years ago, it was
But it feels two minutes behind
I can't get it out of my mind.

I wish I could turn back time
Life is slipping away from me
We are coming to an end
I just need to get round that final bend.

I wish I could turn back time
Why did I tell them?
I could have run
If I had that little boy would be a man.

Adele Wills (12)
Hayesfield School, Bath

Seasons

W inter is the first drop of snow ever to fall,
I ce frozen cold, calm and peaceful like a bird in the wind,
N oise of the rain dripping onto the pure yellow grass,
T rickling of a stream quietly flowing gently,
E vergreen trees still bright and happy in the bitter cold,
R ising of the sun ready for the warmth of spring.

S pring is the first flower opening in bloom,
P etals falling from a blossom tree in the wind,
R ing of the church bells on an early morning,
I cicles have disappeared,
N ewborns make mischief in the fields,
G olden sun appearing for summer.

S ummer is the time for beaches and pools,
U mbrellas in the back of a cupboard, unused,
M elting of an untouched ice cream,
M others watch their children happily play,
E verybody happy in the sun and the sand,
R ain seems like something that does not exist.

A utumn is the golden-brown leaves blowing in the wind,
U p in the sky birds turn to fly south,
T oasty feet warm in comfy socks,
U nder the trees conkers are falling,
M emories of spring and summer fade,
N ow winter is coming, time for cold and rain.

Sadie Thomas (11)
Hayesfield School, Bath

Months

August
She floats through the air and starts plucking flowers
                                        from everywhere.
She looks like a peach and a plum and strawberries too!
Her face golden like the summer sun
Every time she steps on the water, all there is, is a gentle ripple.
But you don't want to make her angry, for if you do, there will be
A hurricane hitting you!

October
I change my clothes
When the leaves change colour
I skip on the rainbow
I sleep on the silky moon
I play on the dew covered grass
I play with the shiny chestnut conkers
And trick people into giving me chocolates
On Hallowe'en
And best of all
It is Grandma's birthday.

December
He lives in a fridge
Wrapped in clothes and blankets of snow
All creatures hide in fear of him, the coldest month of the year.
They lock their doors and need to keep their fires lit.
For when December opens his door all the trees shiver
Covered in frost.
By four o'clock the sun is lost.

Freya Gill (11)
Hayesfield School, Bath

In The Eyes Of A Tiger

I seek the prey ahead of me,
A deer eating grass,
Calm, still and silent,
Like a statue made of brass,
I crouched down low to hide away,
And moved towards my tea,
Keeping my eye on the deer,
That will never again be free,
I pounced and landed on the deer,
And forced it to the ground,
I bit its neck and heard it break,
With a quiet cracking sound,
I tasted blood in my mouth,
It tasted a little sour,
But I carried on eating anyway,
I feasted for an hour.
I left the carcass for the birds,
And turned and walked away,
Happy at my hunting
I was fed for another day!

Tegan Pearce (12)
Hayesfield School, Bath

The Lonely Heart

As she creates an existence aimlessly,
Head in a book, infamously.
No friends, no lovers,
No sisters, no brothers.
Trouble follows her around,
No people to hand.
Far detached from civilisation,
Considered to be a book mutation.
The corridors are empty and so is her heart.
Excels in all subjects especially art.
Allowing her feelings to escape through painting.
Waiting for her moment . . .
A tear slides down her pale cheek,
Anonymous whispers 'disgraceful freak.'
Teachers notice as she shuffles on,
They all look and wonder what is going on.
Little do they realise the horrors of home,
The violence, the pressure, her mother's horrid tone.
All of this treachery has driven her round the bend,
I'm sorry to say this may be the end . . .

Natalie Green (12)
Hayesfield School, Bath

Young Generation

Y outh of today
O ut till all hours
U p and down town
N ever polite
G etting drunk

G ood on the inside
E verybody knows it
N ever want to show it
E ven though they misbehave
R eputation must stand
A lways there
T o remind
I nside
O utside
N ot a chance of fading.

Alice Hughes (12)
Hayesfield School, Bath

The Time Of My Life

That time was great.
That time was brill.
I wish that we could be
Back in that place
Where we were under
That orange maple tree.

Never again will we
Be there, not you,
Not me, no one.
That was then,
This is now.
We cannot go back
For this memory.
     That was:
         The time of my life.

Emily Appleby Matthews (11)
Hayesfield School, Bath

Set Me Free

Dark and cold,
Cramped and not free,
Stuck in a place where no one loves me.
I was once happy, now I am alone,
Far, far away, far away from my home.

I never feared humans, not until this day.
They raised metal monsters and we ran away.
They kill all life, I don't understand,
They destroy all happiness, they take all our land.
I thought they were loving, I thought they were kind,
But animal care to these creatures is blind.

Yet I've heard great stories of humans who care,
With affection and passion, without hate and a glare.
If you have a heart then either care for me,
Or take me back home, please, please set me free.

I want to feel my feet again, I want to see the sun,
I want to prance around again, I want to have some fun!
I want to munch sweet soft grass, I want to see my friends,
And now I fear my once happy life, is about to end.

So if you have a heart, then either care for me,
Or take me back home, please, please set me free!

Rachel Brown (12)
Hayesfield School, Bath

A Fruit Salad

Orange a football you play with on the swaying green grass.
Banana a gun you point at someone who is protected by a mask.
Pear a raindrop falling from the dark gloomy sky.
Apple an ingredient you can put in a tasty soothing pie.
Pineapple a spiky, prickly weapon that could also be called a cactus.

This fruit salad is swarmed with fruits,
So come and join the fiesta and put on your dancing boots!

Alice Derrick (11)
Hayesfield School, Bath

Stage Fright!

Today's the night
I've been looking forward to it all week . . .
I'm not now,
I don't want to go through with it.

Standing in the wing
I can see my mum;
She's got the camera out!

My legs start to shake and I can't stand properly,
I feel faint
And I'm going to fall . . .
Too late, I'm on now!

I stand there shaking like the wind
And I'm standing on a tilt.

Then . . .
I start prancing around,
I'm doing great and everyone was cheering.

And that was the end of my stage fright!

Holly Aldous (12)
Hayesfield School, Bath

Without You

Dear Mummy,
Without you I am like a cow with no milk,
Like a bird with no song,
Right with no wrong.

Without you I am like a hat with no head,
Like a face with no eyes.

Without you I am like an ear with no hearing,
Like a pillow with no duvet.

Without you I am like a dog with no cat,
Like white with no black
Mouse with no rat.

I guess what I'm trying to say Mummy is,
Without you I am nothing.

Love always
Your daughter
Emily.

Jasmine Hazelwood (12)
Hayesfield School, Bath

Food

I love food,
It is so magnificent,
You can have chocolate sauce drizzled over a banana, yum,
Spaghetti Bolognese finished off with a tot of rum,
Delicious juicy strawberries with thick cream on top,
Rice Krispies with milk; snap, crackle, pop!
Hot soup with little bread halves to dip in,
Meringue with fruit compote on, ooo what a sin.

And the meal I look forward to best each year,
Is the hot, scrumptious, lovely Christmas dinner,
You can have roast lamb which has a reddish tint,
Crispy potatoes and some sauce with mint,
Green vegetables and thick, brown gravy which gleams,
And for dessert mince pie with a dollop of ice cream,
But wouldn't you like Christmas dinner every single day?
But you can't until you go through March, April and May!

Alice Howell (12)
Hayesfield School, Bath

My Life As A . . . Lamp Post

I sit watching everything go past,
It all moves but there is no way I can,
Things are touching me, brushing past every second.
Sometimes things bang right into me and I hear them crying,
And then someone taking their hand and walking into the distance.

I feel so alone, never been able to make a single sound, but I hear
All ever spoken.
Birds land on my head and workmen fiddle with my fuses
But I still glow at night.
Lighting up the streets, except for me it has only ever been the one
on North River Street.
At night I sleep but am still aware of movement and sound,
I can hear happy families sitting around a table and eating the dinner
of their life.
I can never eat, I can never drink, I can never enjoy life.

I have no life, just to light streets and die.
I wish I could eat and drink and talk but no, I will just glow, break
Down and be forgotten about, for I am a lamp post, and just grow
old and rusty.

Kristina Hunt (11)
Hayesfield School, Bath

No Words

No words can describe the emotions of Man,
No gossip of the day,
No sunshine on the misty fields,
No children out to play.

Empty roads and deserted parks
And cars with no bright lights,
Houses with darkened rooms,
Light days and duller nights.

Grey-blue skies, smoky towns,
Dead, brown, bare gardens,
Disfunctional dark street lamps,
Scared silenced pardons.

Staring faces,
Untied laces,
Finished races,
Heavy paces.

No words can describe the emotions of Man
No gossip of the day,
No sunshine on the misty fields,
No children out to play.

Imogen Jones (12)
Hayesfield School, Bath

Through No One's Eyes

Looking,
For the impossible dream,
Seeking,
For the things I haven't seen
Hiding,
From myself inside
Watching,
From the other side
Weeping,
Why am I here at all?
Thinking,
If I die, will anyone care?

Crying,
Tears streaming that I cannot stop,
Sobbing,
I have no point, no reason in life,
Blinking,
My sorrow means nothing,
Staring,
Why keep me here on Earth?
Widening,
As fever and coldness surround me,
Closing
Eternal sleep.

Daisy Edwards (12)
Hayesfield School, Bath

Why Don't You Love Me?

My life started with a human
As many cat lives do
Only he abused me
And across the room I flew.

He kicked me and he punched me
And when moved away
I made a new life on the streets
I lived another day.

It wasn't as good as I imagined
And to make it very blunt
I hardly ever had some food
As I hadn't learned to hunt.

Also cats on the street ain't friendly
Or as cute as they appear
I spent the next few years of my life
Living in secret fear.

One day when I was hunting
A car stopped by my side
The hands of a human grabbed me
Hauling me inside.

They took me to their home
Gave me food and a place to nap
Now I lead a happy life
On someone else's lap.

Kitty Cordero (12)
Hayesfield School, Bath

In This Life What Am I?

At the moment I am very small
Just turning from a tiny ball
Sprouting out to breathe the air
I've had a long wait, it wasn't fair
We're popping up all over the place
Winter's gone, no trace
I am in spring.

I can see nearly all the world
The sun's beating down, I'm turning yellow
In the heat, the horses - how they mellow
Swaying along in the cool breeze
I can smell something - it's the seas
I am in the luscious summer.

I am turning crisp red and falling, falling
The winter howls are calling, calling
Dropping, dropping I am on the ground
My friends also fall turning round and round
That's it for a while then - no more up at the top
I have entered autumn.

Brr it's cold, I'm all trampled and wet
The rain is falling and now it's set
I'm blowing away, farewell I say
Here comes winter.

I am small but very high
Seeing the world flying by
Birds up here, people down there
Insects flying through the air
I am green, yellow, brown and red
What am I it must be said?
A leaf.

Eleanor Hall (12)
Hayesfield School, Bath

Darkness

As you cried in my arms,
As you fell from grace
I surrendered to my darkness.

As my heart is bleeding
And my eyes are blind
I succumb to the darkness,
Not reached by your light.

As your heart ceases to beat
In my bloody hands,
As the peace is written on your face,
My heart is cloven in two.

As all light leaves me,
As my darkness swallows me,
I feel the sweet pain,
Taste the familiar blood,
Feel the life leave me.

Lily Jennings (12)
Hayesfield School, Bath

Nan

We think of you with love each day,
Things you used to do and used to say,
They bring a smile then a tear,
And wishing you were here,
Deep in our hearts, memories are kept,
Of a special nan we will never forget.

We know you're so special
To us and others too,
We wish that other people
Would be just like you.

You're in our hearts
And always will be,
We shall miss seeing you,
You're our gold, our star,
Our treasure forever.

Laura Taylor (12)
Hayesfield School, Bath

My Ferrets

Honey.
Honey is the smallest, although she's very tough,
She tells the other ferrets off, when they're playing rough.

Buddy.
Buddy is albino and very playful too,
He wants to run and jump about, all day and all night through.

Bruno.
Bruno is a rascal and often is a pain,
He's the only ferret that I know, who really likes the rain.

Scampi.
Scampi's very gentle and likes to snuggle in,
But when we let them out to play, he jumps straight in the bin.

Toffee.
Toffee is the youngest and really cute too,
As he is cinnamon, and likes to nibble you.

Chip.
Chippy has now left us and gone to a good place,
But when he was much younger, he loved a game of 'chase'.

Sparkie.
Sparks has also gone now but loved to have a hug,
He also liked hot chocolate, from deep inside your mug.

These are all my ferrets and I love them all so much,
They're loving and so sweet and they're all so soft to touch.

Gemma Eades (12)
Hayesfield School, Bath

My House

My home is a big mad house
Full of love and kindness
Home is a giant's hand
Giving me warmth and shelter
My house is a zoo full of sweet rescued animals
My home is a calm beach
With rough waves and full of screams
I love my house!

Sophie McInnes (12)
Hayesfield School, Bath

I Stand Alone . . .

I stand alone like a desolate beach,
My private hole undiscovered and secret.
I stand alone harbouring my solitude,
Staring and standing on tall windy cliffs.
I stand alone not lonely or longing,
But fierce and mysterious,
Unknown and alone . . .

Gina Ling (12)
Hayesfield School, Bath

Into The Unknown

Into the unknown
Plunging deep, hurtling forward,
Into pure existence.
Trapped inside a glowing ball of indigo blue,
There is no reason, no explanation for anything.

Into the unknown
A new identity, new life,
Time slips away, you are stillness,
Thoughts clamour and float around
The crest of an Atlantic wave forms.

Into the unknown,
Passing silent lakes,
Sparkling with ultimate happiness,
Over mountains, forests,
Questioning what comes next.

Waterfalls crash around,
But yet there is still silence,
And a shuddering from the pit of your stomach,
Life flashes everywhere,
You continue

Into the unknown
There seems to be no light,
Just pure nothingness penetrating your senses,
Simple delights of the day,
Gone, no more,
New surroundings push and shove,
But none are remembered.

Into the unknown,
A blank sheet of paper,
Stretching and stretching,
Into all eternity,
Endless space, seems so big,
You so small,
A speck of dust.

Into the unknown,
A scream. A cry,
Fades into the distance,
As if it were never there,
With no one you know to hear it,
All sounds seem irrelevant,
Smells cease to exist,
And sights flash, and waver,
No great memories there

Into the unknown,
Back where you came from,
Seems now so strange,
As did your home,
Deep inside a cold mountain range,
You now seem so alone,
But back in the busy noisy city,
You're comfortable,
Known . . .

Helen Tatlow (11)
High School for Girls, Gloucester

Emotions

Do you feel?
Trapped like a caged lovebird longing for its mate
Or scared like a young tiger cub whose mother has just become
A fancy fur coat.
Perhaps?
Insecure like a child who has just figured out that their daddy's not
Coming home.
Or different like a thistle laying within a beautiful English rose garden.

Are you feeling?
Elegant like a swan sitting gracefully on the calm waters of the lake
And loved like the first batch of freshly made cookies,
One autumn morning.
Or maybe you feel?
Free like the gentle winds that blow
And proud like the golden eagle perched high, overlooking the
Grand Canyon below.
I know I do . . .

Katie Rees (14)
Newent Community School, Newent

White Is The Snow

White is the snow, twirling down
Lands on a tree, hard and brown.

Brown is the tree, waving to the night
Touching the sky, grey with no light.

Grey is the sky, on a frosty day
Sun peeking through, a golden ray.

Yellow is the sun, hot and bright
Next to a bird, food in its sight.

Red is the bird, flying around
Spots a worm, on the ground.

Pink is the worm, covered in snow,
Next to a tree, where the branches flow.

Kelly O'Neill (11)
Oldfield School, Bath

The Ever Changing World

Lush, green grass,
Bronzed trees,
Bright yellow sun
And golden leaves.

Smoky blue sky,
Crisp fresh air,
Shiny feathers around me,
Everywhere!

Lazy days,
Lounging around,
Easy life having fun!

This is how it used to be!

But now . . .

Crunchy crisp wrappers,
Greasy chips,
Grimy ash
I hate all this.

Stinking smoke,
Muggy air,
Killer fumes
Everywhere!

This is what we've done!

We can make it better,
Working together,
Together with friends,
In just a little time.

Things will be back to normal,
Bright and breezy,
It'll benefit everyone,
To turn this grubby life around.

Esther Docherty (11)
Oldfield School, Bath

Rose Colour Glasses

Through rose colour glasses, what can you see?
A tree full of life.
The environment's now changing,
From bright to dark.
What used to be couldn't stay the same,
If we make an effort what do you think?
When I put on my glasses,
I see deer in fields and woods,
Playing hide-and-seek.
When I take them off, I see
The wild has changed to a wreck and a junk yard.
This used to be a beautiful countryside,
With flowers and ponds,
Admired and divine.
The world is on the edge of disgrace,
No one will stop littering, crisps packets
Chucked, cans and wrappers thrown.
Keep the world tidy and everyone will have
Their bit to share.

Ashley Souch (11)
Oldfield School, Bath

Smile

You smile at me,
But I know it's a safety net.
It's because you don't know what to do, or what to say
It's awkward.

I smile back,
But it's because
I want to be loved by you
And you know it.

So your smile changes,
Into what I know is deception.
A trap.
Because your lips are the shape of deceit,
And your eyes are doing the talking.

Tell me,
When will it be that you smile properly?
Not to pass the time or deceive me.
When will you smile like you love me?

Fiona Stainer (14)
St Gregory's Catholic College, Bath

The Hanged Man

Wasteland
Gleams, chemical
Cleans, hovers, hung
In the air.

Suffocates,
Chokes, throttled
Swinging
Helpless as a child
In the broken breeze.

Man, no eyes
Tongue - mouth
Open like gate
To the twisted garden.

Proud, too proud
Wicked, sinful one.

Stumps squat on his hands,
His fingers gone, gold ring,
Hold the magpie safe.

Slowly now, quietly now
Bother nobody
They never do make noise,
Apart from the shouting first
Screams of a dead man echo.

In silence

The hanged man is dead.

Danielle Vrublevskis (14)
St Gregory's Catholic College, Bath

Smile

The muscles contract and relax,
To form the most beautiful smile,
On the most beautiful face,
The perfection is just your style.

It dazzles everywhere you go,
Shining pearly white teeth,
Luring everyone into thinking,
That you couldn't give them grief.

But I know you and I know you will,
I've seen that smile hurt and betray,
Setting traps like a spider does,
Smiling until you have your prey . . .

Then that smile turns to a smirk,
The teeth turn into fangs,
With every cruel word you will destroy,
Whenever someone tries to hold your hand.

That smile is your deadly weapon,
It gives you anything, anybody you want,
A simple grin and they're all yours,
It's a talent that you flaunt . . .

Some people don't look past the surface,
But I look at you for a long while
And I see the cruelty, rejections, the lies and spite,
And I know I can't give into your smile.

Anna Moon (15)
St Gregory's Catholic College, Bath

Angel Eyes

When she holds you in your stare,
Your whole life pulls together.
Every person that she meets,
Never will forget her.

Soft skin, red lips, even beautiful hair,
But as to the sparkle in her eyes,
Nothing can compare.

When all seems dead - no hope is alive,
Light shines from her angel eyes.

The emotion of all her years
Swim deep beneath the brown
Happiness, joy - pain and fear

One look can make you internally warm
Safe from the pain in the world around.
Harsh words spoken - evil scorn.

When nothing seems right,
You want to break down and cry,
Light shines from her angel eyes.

Instead of soaring in the skies,
Here on Earth she gets us through.
Love, warmth and strength pour from her
Angel eyes.

Evie Netto (14)
St Gregory's Catholic College, Bath

Tears Of Rain

Rain is merely the tears of the past
Tears that have fallen from misty eyes
Tiny warm drops that grazed one cheek
Bring sorrow to a warm grey sky.

They fall, fall,
Lightly first as if with shame
Growing deeper, more persistent still,
Hammering hard against the pane.

Dampened spirits will hide away
As the sky cries itself to sleep
Without shelter I am soaked to the skin
I cannot move for the puddles at my feet.

In a single drop my soul is reflected
I take cover so no one will see
After the wave has passed, nothing will have changed
After the storm I will still be me.

Should the tears of my present become the rain in your future,
Rain, will be inescapable.

Helen Brown (15)
Sidcot School, Winscombe

Missing Identity

It moves like fog,
Searching for someone, something
It glides through dark alleyways
Like a ghost in a huge mansion.
It's sad and lonely,
It is invisible but still unique.
At least until it finds it
But where could it be nobody knows
It runs, it goes
Where? Nobody knows.

Lily Hughes (11)
Stroud High School, Stroud

The Family Photo Album

As I look through my pages,
At lots of ages,
I see some happy sights . . .

Grandma Madge and Uncle Bill
Little baby cousin, Will,
Kissing sister, Millie too.

Seasides, fairgrounds, first days at school,
Mum and Dad looking a fool,
And Auntie Bessie with her bassoon.

I creak and squeak,
I feel weak,
But these sights make me happy.

Tom on sports day fast as a truck
Cousin Billy's first hair cut,
And many more wonderful sights.

My pages are torn,
My covers on the floor,
I'm sticky with fingerprints too.

But do I care?
I love to share
The memories of the family.

The photos then come to a stop
My memory starts to blot,
I suddenly feel old . . .

Natasha Hole (11)
Stroud High School, Stroud

My Life In A Fairy Tale

My too long hair is holding my prince
He loves it, I hate it.
He thinks my hair shines like the sun
I think my hair is like a bale of straw
But all the same I think it will help us.
I will get away from this deep dark place,
And I will go far, far away.

I have finally found a way out from this dark place,
I will have nothing, but my prince and our love.
I personally never thought I would say this but,
I love my hair!

With practically no hair compared to before
For I cut it off whilst my prince tried to stop me.
With his sharpest sword I raised my hand and slashed.
My hair in a plait magically turned into a rope.

But as we descended we heard a cry of
'You can't do this to me'
Oh dear, it's my minder coming to check on me
But my dear one fought bravely against them
And we managed to get away.

We went to my prince's castle to get married
And within three days
My long-lost mother and father came to stay.

I am now the happiest I have ever been in my life,
Everything is perfect.

And we lived happily ever after . . .

Megan Belcher (11)
Stroud High School, Stroud

An Old Person

Like an animal's cage,
No windows, one door
Brings up fresh rage,
You're cared for no more.

You're losing your sight,
You're hunched over, not tall,
You can't reach the light,
Like a young animal, you call.

A bright light comes to help,
For a moment life's alright,
The door slams shut,
Your breathing is tight.

How long? How long? Will you last?
An old photo album,
Remembers your wonderful past.
But you wait for your last day to come.

Jessica Jackson (11)
Stroud High School, Stroud

The Dark Coal Mine - Haikus

I dig and I dig
Everyone chipping away
In the dark coal mine.

A small container
Holds the light, the light we need
But still it is dark.

Only some of us
Others are on strike, just us
Working all alone.

Too many gasses
Too many people dying
When will my time come?

Hannah Oulsnam (11)
Stroud High School, Stroud

The Abandoned Dog

The blinding snow sweeps the streets,
I cower beneath a battered box,
Longing for food and comfort and warmth,
But nobody seems to care.

Brimming dustbins beckon and call,
I rummage through bottles and empty tins,
For last night's chicken and stale bread,
Tasteless, disgusting and dull.

Darkness brings the fiendish rats
And foxes that prowl the empty streets,
Slinking through the shadows like thieves on a job,
Scouring the alleys for food.

Alone in the gloom I whimper with fear,
The cold bites my frozen paws,
I cry for home, my family, my basket,
But the night shows no sympathy.

By day I wander the lonely town,
Begging and whining for tasty scraps.
Cries of 'Leave, you dirty dog!'
Follow wherever I go.

I never cease to wonder why
I was left to lead this lonely life,
Dragged from the car at the side of the road,
Lost, alone and confused.

I know that someday someone will come,
And wake me up from this nightmare world,
And take me in with loving arms,
That hope will never drown.

Rebecca Field (11)
Stroud High School, Stroud

Why?

They want me to be famous,
I want to be a nurse.
They say you're someone or no one,
I say is there no in-between,
They think I should be the same take the fame,
I think I don't want to be the same couldn't bear the fame.

Why can't I create my own identity?
Why can't they leave me alone?

They want me to wear Dolce and Gabana,
I want to wear H&M and Gap,
They say I should be somebody,
I say I'll be somebody's whatever.
They think I should sing and dance,
I think I should do something worthwhile.

Why can't I create my own identity?
Why can't they leave me alone?

Robyn Overfield-Whitear (12)
Stroud High School, Stroud

Identity

Identity, is it something you hate and do not want?
Or something you want and will keep forever.
Whatever you call it you have it.
May you be white or copper skinned
Do you have blue, brown or green eyes with brown,
Blonde or red hair, it does not matter.
You have it, identity is your life,
Your characteristics form your face, I am like a joker in a
Pack of cards no one wants me but they have me.
They don't know that I can win the game.
You can't buy me, trade me or change me.
I am identity and I am what you make me.

Anne Townsend (11)
Stroud High School, Stroud

Abandoned Dog

I sit on the road scared and alone,
Hoping that one day I will go home.

Cars pass me in every direction,
No humans, no one would give me
Affection.

Lots of people stand and stare,
I cry at the end of my voice,
I think to myself, *no one cares.*

I wish I could find my owners again,
I'm cold and wet, and I'm old, I'm ten.

I'm starving hungry and I'm becoming thin,
'Any scraps will do,' I say as I search
Through a bin.

Holly Histed (11)
Stroud High School, Stroud

On The Streets

Lost and abandoned
A cute little ball of fluff
Alone on the streets.

An old cardboard box
My kitten's luxury bed
With newspaper rug.

Behind the baker's
Mouldy bread - the gourmet meal
Foul smells fill the air.

My poor sad kitten
A dark alley - home sweet home
Dirt adorns the floor.

Cat Leach (11)
Stroud High School, Stroud

Stray

My worn paws scuff the ground,
As I search for a scrap of meat,
The dusty cars and their roaring sound,
Almost hit me in the blurry heat.

I wish for somewhere to sleep,
I wish for a safe, loving home,
But with just matted fur I have nothing to give,
So I'm thrown out and left alone.

But soon I spot some milk in the shade,
I shoot over like a bullet from a gun,
Then I see a cat, my dreams fade
I limp away as the blood dries in the sun.

Won't anyone adopt me?
I am tattered as an old mat,
I'm rake-thin as you can see,
But inside I'm a kind, lonely cat.

Georgia Saunders (11)
Stroud High School, Stroud

Teddy Bear

Loved and cuddled every day
He takes me everywhere,
Taken to the zoo,
And dragged up the stair.

But as he begins to get older
He cuddles me less and less,
He drops me in a muddy puddle
Even in dog's mess.

He still puts me in the washing machine
But forgets to bring me out,
I'm like a crumpled piece of paper,
Crumpled without a doubt.

I'm put up high on a shelf
They want to throw me away,
They don't like me no more,
Oh well, I've had my day.

Alice Jollans (11)
Stroud High School, Stroud

Where Am I?

I scratch hard on the wooden door,
On a cold winter's day, cold crisp snow falls gently,
I shiver,
I feel alone, abandoned, devastated,
Oh why please let me in!

Are they abandoning me?
Leaving me in the cold crisp snow,
Cold as ice?
Like throwing away a banana skin,
Or shutting the door to loneliness.

I am cold, very cold,
Dying in this snow,
Shall I go or shall I stay?
I think I will go!
I wander in the streets of London.

Looking for a home, any home,
At last I start to give up hope,
When suddenly, I see,
A mysterious looking man,
Just the one for me!

I run over, quickly like cheetahs after their prey,
He wraps me up in his jumper,
And takes me to his house,
It was love at first sight,
Hope has come on Christmas Eve!

Sophie Milner (11)
Stroud High School, Stroud

Politics Vs Me (Using My Senses)

They've built up such a stereotype
Of 'The youth of today'.
The blameless are standing here
What else can we say?

They never stop debating
Commanding military personnel.
Whilst we take in the danger
They think we cannot smell.

They're tearing up the planet
And trying to agree,
Whilst we absorb the beauty
They think we cannot see.

It's just lie after lie,
And deal after deal.
Where has the ancient trust gone that
They think we cannot feel?

They're setting an example
With an element of fear.
'Try to protect the innocent,' they say
They think we cannot hear.

I can't explain my feelings.
The planet's in disgrace.
Now understand the bitterness
That we will have to face.

Esther Harding (14)
Stroud High School, Stroud

Homeless

I am living on the street,
I have nowhere to go,
I have nothing to eat,
I always feel low.

I feel so empty,
Like nothing in a tin,
A box can't be homely,
I should go to that inn.

I go to the inn for a night,
I get food and a bed,
I feel just right,
As I snuggle up in my shed.

I wake up in the morning,
I am a happy man,
People around me who are caring,
Trying to help all they can.

Annabel McCrindle (11)
Stroud High School, Stroud

The Old Teddy Bear

I was loved and cuddled for years and years,
I was there to help her fight her fears,
I loved Sarah,
And she loved me,
Together we made a great family.

But as Sarah started to get older and older,
Her love for me grew colder and colder,
I was up high
And I wondered why,
Please don't leave me up here.

I was left up there for years and years,
No one to help me fight my fears,
I loved Sarah,
But she didn't love me
That's the end of our family!

Megan Jones (11)
Stroud High School, Stroud

Loved?

L oved? I think not, or I would not be in this hell.
O ver and over again I do my same routine. Miaow, big eyes,
   Paw on cage door.
C ourse it has not worked yet or I would be at my home all snug
   And warm. Not here where it is as miserable as sin.
K illed! That is how I feel. Dead inside, so lonely, so empty.
E verything around me is melting, fading away. My fur
   As rough as sandpaper, my eyes drooping.
D ear dear, they say cats have nine lives, although I have
   Not even lived my first.

U nfortunate, unlucky, unloved. If I wrote an autobiography
   Those are the only three words that would belong to my book.
P erhaps I was not made for the high class living and only for
   This cat pound. For now I will just rest, perfect my routine,
   And hope that my future owners walk through these doors
   Sometime soon.

Holly Davis-Grant (12)
Stroud High School, Stroud

Lonely Old Lady

My life is so boring, just sitting in my chair
No one comes to visit me, no one really cares.

My husband has long passed away
My children are all far away
I struggle on every day.

Have no one to talk to, no one to tell
I am as lonely as the last toy on the shelf.

I am very ill, getting weaker every day
As I hobble down the high street
No one turns their head to see.

Cooling cold shivers my spine
Ending, life ending all the time.

Memories all lost
Like sand flowing fast through my fingers
I will be forgotten
Not be remembered
As I pass away, Heaven lingers.

Tabitha Haldane-Unwin (11)
Stroud High School, Stroud

A Stray Dog

I was once in a house,
In a cosy bed,
Children around me,
A new baby came,
There wasn't enough room for me.

A stray lost dog,
I looked rake-thin,
Nowhere to go,
Cold, lonely and abandoned,
In an old box on the street,
Alone like a beggar.

I hear a young, small cry,
Like a bird crying help,
I look around then I see,
A small puppy next to me,
I now have a friend to comfort me,
Now as cosy and as warm as I will ever be.

Cuddled up cosy and content,
I feel warm, guarded and safe.

Joanna Judd (12)
Stroud High School, Stroud

Celebrity Crisis

I wake up, everything's normal,
Everything the same, similar, safe life
Until I leave the front door . . .

Snap, flash, 'Look this way,'
The paparazzi pounce like panthers on their prey,
Me.

I dash to my car,
Like a bullet being fired from a gun,
'Go, go after her,' I hear them cry.

I get to my destination -
The mall is a sea of photographers and fans
Signing autographs here and there.

A press conference next,
Being attacked from every angle
And being sold for thousands.

At the end of the day,
I'm adored by millions, loved by millions
But am I happy, is it worth it?

Danielle Munday (12)
Stroud High School, Stroud

Diary

I am your confidante, your friend,
The keeper of your secrets
You can always count on me
I am your history, your past, your memory
Not what's going to be
Although each page, like the Mayfly, dies
At the end of each day
It's content, your thoughts cannot be
Thrown away.

My sheets are rather special, a record of your life
Each one tells a story
Adventures and troubles, smiles and tears
The truth in all its glory
I hold your feelings, like your heart
Your memories, the feelings are never far apart.

I am always close by, a shoulder to cry on,
Someone that shares in your joy
Although just a book it is never too hard to listen to you
I can be there, it is not the case that I do not care
I like to help, I am happy too!
You think I have no understanding like a newborn child,
But I do, I have ears, it's just that my response is very mild.

And in years to come I will still be here to remind you of what's been,
A distant sound in the far-off past
The book that shaped who you've become - the
Script, the scene, the cast.
Hurting, healing, healthy, happy or not
I'm everything that's been before, I'm really all you've got.

Rachel Matthews (11)
Stroud High School, Stroud

The Book On The Shelf

I sat on the shelf,
Dusty and moth-eaten

Like an old man,
An old man slowly rotting

What would it be like to be touched?
Maybe even seen

To be read,
To finally have someone turn your pages

Or even say that it was good
I will probably never know

I was as worthless as a dust mite,
A maggot,

Or some kind of head louse
Maybe even a germ

Yet worth so much more.
Right?

I had no expectations
Or ambitions

Apart from to be opened,
Just opened.

Opened by someone, anyone
Is that too much to ask?

All they need is imagination,
It's only imagination

That's all you need,
But a liking for adventure never hurt anyone.

Amy Watson (11)
Stroud High School, Stroud

Living On The Streets

Wandering aimlessly,
Conscious of nothing but my need for food
I am hungry, so hungry.

I find a dry corner,
Put down my box, and my bowl, just in case,
Settle down for the night.

Darkness falls,
Like a big black blanket over me,
Obscuring my view.

Then the cold hits,
A bitter wind whistles through the streets,
It begins to drizzle.

I wake up cold, wet and stiff
But everywhere outside is fresh and clean,
The rain has washed away the night.

People begin to flood the streets,
They seem full of happiness and joy,
Why do they glance down when they pass me?

I rise painfully,
Only to begin my cycle again,
Only to wander aimlessly.

Rebecca McKie (12)
Stroud High School, Stroud

Identity?

Nobody knows, nobody cares,
Stuck here, singled out,
Left alone, no defences,
Lost my family, lost my home,
To the menacing destruction,
That has long foregone,
But the scars are there; the pain is there;

Along with rank rubbish, along with dirt,
People can laugh, people can sneer, but,
Please help me . . .
Please save me . . .
The explosion was jeopardy that brought death;
It had no mercy,
It had no love,
Only anger, anger . . . and hate;

I screamed for life, I screamed my name,
Like a banshee in distress,
I screamed until my voice was hoarse,
But I am not unique,
I am something that no one cares about,
Stuck here, singled out,
Left alone, no defences,
I am not unique . . .
I am nothing . . .

Prudence Morgan-Wood (12)
Stroud High School, Stroud

The Writer's Chorus

I fill minds with doom, gloom and laughter
My name will exist forever and after
Words are my mind, my soul and my heart
They flow through my veins, they are my art.

I write for my children
I write for my wife
I write for the world
I write for my life.

My head is a cave filled with raging black ocean
My words are a fever, swaying with motion
My soul opens and pours onto paper
I am whisked down from the Earth into gaping craters.

I write for my children
I write for my wife
I write for the world
I write for my life.

Letters are beautiful wondrous things
Of murders and lovers and pigs with wings
A universe is created, a magical land
With deep black sky and ancient sands.

I write for my children
I write for my wife
I write for the world
I write for my life.

Matilda McMorrow (11)
Stroud High School, Stroud

Laments Of A Lion

My claws unsheathe as I pace my cage
I let out a cry of unspoken rage

Eyes close as I shake my mane
So long since I ran on the wide open plain

Their two-legged cubs, wide-eyed they stare
Narrow my eyes in sadness and despair

Their bushes and trees unreal, so fake
My memories of a vast blue lake

They open the cage, hear me roar
How long since I saw the fine birds soar?

Then I growl for all to hear
No twitching jackrabbit or terrified deer

The meat it stinks of their unwashed hand
Faraway dreams of faraway lands

My coat dulls as my memories fade
No towering cliff or shady glade

How can I have sunk so low?
Where is the sun's golden glow?

Once I was great, I was the king
Now I am trapped, a mere plaything

Why am I here, trapped like prey?
I will escape, I long for that day.

Amy Clark (11)
Stroud High School, Stroud

Fame

I don't want to get out of my stretch limousine,
But I totter about on my sky-high high heels.
Flash bulbs explode like lightning in my face,
Momentarily blinding me as I stagger down the red carpet,
As I almost fall flat.
The super-tight dress isn't helping either,
I feel like I've been squeezed down a rubber tube,
I can barely walk anyway,
I want to go home.
My amazing new hairstyle is stuck to my designer lipstick,
And the reporters scream at me to
'Give them a smile'
'Give them a twirl'
And are still insisting I look fabulous
Do I?

Holly Paveling (11)
Stroud High School, Stroud

The Battlefield

The battlefield here it comes,
You can't hear your own lungs.
The roar and grunt of people's homes
Being trashed and falling down each of the rungs.
The battlefield, ouch it kills,
To be watching the entire race that fills.
Just leave them there lying
The back teeth tying all around,
It makes you see red everywhere
Just don't go as your cage will be more than rattled.

Liam Swattridge (13)
The Crypt School, Gloucester

Global Warming

Peaceful.
Just lying here, floating
With no worries.

Antarctica, always quiet and serene
But bit by bit, I begin to dream.
Water rising, taking over,
Slowly killing, it's all over.
Pollution, cars and mess,
All a pointless, agonising distress.
Fumes and gases and hotter world,
Polar bears tightly curled
Burning crusade, I begin to melt,
Slowly drowning, suffocated: a smouldering belt,
Water rising, land retreating,
Earth's resources, slowly shrinking.

What's the point of this excruciating pain?
Let's stop it now, and make it tame.
We started this chaos, so let's finish this madness,
Before the insanity, causes much sadness.

Disturbed.
Drowning, slowly, much torture.
But why?

Luke Holbrook (14)
The Crypt School, Gloucester

Global Warming

Smouldering, suffering, searing.
Destruction, disaster, death.
Burning, blistering, boiling.
It is upon us,
It is with us,
It is now.
We are in a greenhouse,
Will you open the door?

Sam Backhouse (14)
The Crypt School, Gloucester

The Religious War

The politicians row
The people listen
The words fight
And their shiny rings glisten.

It is about religion
The faith of war
But no one is certain
As they leave through the door.

The faiths wear symbols
Show the devotion of Man
Leaders try to bring communities together
But only we can.

Headscarves, necklaces
Turbans and rings
Payos and skullcaps
Among several other things.

Why the hatred?
Why the spite?
Aren't we all human?
In the presence of God's might?

If we all stand united:
United as one,
We could get through
The harshness of Man.

Mark Bates (14)
The Crypt School, Gloucester

The Creature In The Snow

Have you ever wondered?
Have you ever dreamed?
About another picture
About another scene.

I can now tell you
All that I know
For I was once
The creature in the snow.

The winter is cold
The winter is bare
But no one complained
No one does care.

The forest was my wisdom
The forest was my home
All creatures were my friends
All of them I know.

The strange men came
Equipped with saws
Down go the trees
'Timber' they roar.

Don't let this happen
Save all you know
For once I was
The creature in the snow.

Ben Russell (11)
The Crypt School, Gloucester

Children Of War

The troops go to war,
Just as they've done for years before.

Why are we fighting, why won't they listen?
Is there something we are all missing?

The bloodshed, terror panic, stench of war,
For king and country we bravely fought before.

The images we see up on a screen,
Rubble, ashes where homes have been.

The poignant small shoe left in the dust
Children screaming for a crust.

They are the innocent with lives ripped away,
We blindly follow our leaders and obey.

Have we still learnt nothing from the past?
Fighting, punishing, maiming to the last.

Is the legacy we leave our children, more war?
They are pure, we corrupt them for sure.

But we all have a goal, to protect those we love
And pray to whoever our god is above.

These emotions for each of us are strong and true,
There is hope war will stop if they love their children too.

Matthew Gowell (15)
The Crypt School, Gloucester

Untitled

The grey swirling plumes,
Waft into the skies,
Eating away at the shield,
That protects us from our father.
We are terrified of death, but
Force it upon ourselves.

George Wright (14)
The Crypt School, Gloucester

To Death

You followed us into battle and war,
You took our loved ones away from us.
Why Death? Why did you do that?

You made the young fall to rise no more,
You took them from their mothers when they were born.
Why Death? Why did you do that?

You took the elderly from us with no notice,
You took the quiet and made them silent.
Why Death? Why did you do that?

You do all this every day,
You take them from us,
You remove the wanted,
Replace them with nothing.

Why Death? Why don't you take me?

Martin Parker (14)
The Crypt School, Gloucester

The Soldiers

Blinded by propaganda
Fooled by constant banter
Cheated by mindless chatter
Do they deserve this?

Death was almost there
Frightened by a constant stare
Taunted by the mocking gunshots
Is this fair?

Now we are at peace
So many are deceased
They are the brave soldiers who gave their lives
Enabling us to continue to survive.

Kane Hazard (13)
The Crypt School, Gloucester

The Forgotten Child

She was left there in the cold and rain
But no one felt nor heard her pain
She had no one, no one
No one to turn to, no one to look after her.
Cold and hungry she knelt down
On her rough, harsh floor she knelt
She was sodden and perishing
She was left there, left to cry
Left to cry, and left to die.

On her own in the cold and rain
No one felt nor heard her pain
Her spirit was crushed forever
She was alone in the frost
Her heart was turning, changing to stone
Would she be found, saved
Or just left in the cold and rain
She was left there, left to cry
Left to cry and left to die.

James Keasley (13)
The Crypt School, Gloucester

Bovad?

Ice caps melting every day,
Solutions getting further away,
Islands flooded by next May.

Adults, children, getting shot,
Both in wars and also not,
Bush is helping? Eh? What?

Children dying, AIDS, no food.
Oxfam show pictures, disturbing, crude,
Still we do nothing they're lying, dying, nude.

Stefan Quarry (14)
The Crypt School, Gloucester

Famine

This is a problem,
That sweeps the world,
It makes people sad,
Who wish to be hurled.

Nobody likes it,
They'd wish it be gone,
It is a serious problem
Which must be decreased down to none.

This is famine you see,
It is part of life,
Nobody likes it,
It's trouble and strife.

We all want it to go,
It strikes us down,
Lots of people suffer
Who'd rather drown.

Jacob Prosser (14)
The Crypt School, Gloucester

The Earth

The ice,
Thawing,
The forests,
Falling,
The planet,
Mourning,
Imprisoned in its smothering shield.

Dominic Harrison (15)
The Crypt School, Gloucester

A Countdown To Destruction

In seconds, any town, any city or any country,
Can be destroyed by Man's destructive lust,
A fearsome terror that falls from the skies
And reduces all within miles to dust.

America, Britain, Russia, France, China,
The five nuclear weapons' states,
India, Pakistan and North Korea,
With their yet undecided fates.

And yet who are America,
To judge the rights of others,
With their 5,000 strong arsenal,
To use on their fellow brothers?

And then there are those under suspicion,
Iran, and their new nuclear program,
They insist it for the good of their people,
Or is it just yet another scam?

In a single press of a button,
A country could always fall,
To the metal angels of death,
The warheads that stand so tall.

A nuclear war becomes more likely,
With every passing day,
It would cause a nuclear winter,
Then all of the world would pay.

With every country developing nuclear weapons,
Soon all will have at least one,
Now it's only a matter of time,
The countdown has already begun . . .

Stuart Andrews (15)
The Crypt School, Gloucester

Raging Liars Smoking

This is a call
From all those who you affect,
To show what addiction does to you -
The other things you regret.

Raging liars smoking,
Digging away
Because they feel insane.
Raging liars burning,
Light up their day -
Willing to risk the rain.

Do you run outside,
With your excuses of
Endless abuses
To your mind?
Then do you scream inside,
Taking your chances for
Meaningless rushes
To your mind?

Raging liars smoking,
Digging away
Because then they'll feel the same.
Raging liars burning
Light up their day -
Willing to risk the rain.

'I need some fresh air' -
Is that your lie for
Endless excuses
To your mind?

Toby Ellis (14)
The Crypt School, Gloucester

The Youth

I am a dog
I live in a house
I eat and I sleep
I don't do much else
I'm lazy.

Once in a while
I go for a walk
I run for an hour
I sleep for a day
I'm lazy.

Every night I eat
Afterwards I sleep
That's all I do
I eat and I sleep
I'm lazy.

Cameron Ramsey (15)
The Crypt School, Gloucester

The Meaning Of Life

I guess we will never know,
Maybe it's God staging one big show,
It's a hard question to answer,
Are we here to catch the deadly cancer,
Is it a trial,
For which there can be no denial,
The meaning of life,
A question that has caused so much strife.

Tom Longley (14)
The Crypt School, Gloucester

Forgotten

His eyes opened;
Another day
Another day of nothingness
Why was he forgotten?
Why is he left?
His glazed eyes, the shut doors,
Into a world of nothing.

Why did he wake?
The world does nothing
Nothing but pass him by and forget
Forget the emptiness
Forget the meaning
The world does nothing
But sit and watch him fade
Into the emptiness of his life . . .

Timothy Keasley (13)
The Crypt School, Gloucester

Bloodshed

2006, and the Earth's just begun,
But we're killing our paradise,
Sat under the sun,
Tin boxes on wheels, racing about,
Eating our oils.
When will we run out?
And when we do, how will we survive?
Without our tin boxes with wheels to drive.
Drills whizzing, pumps drinking,
Sucking the Earth's blood,
Two-legged leeches,
Who moan when prices go up.

Tom Badger (14)
The Crypt School, Gloucester

The Chills Of Winter

The first break of spring,
The sun yawning, lazily breaking away
From the icy grasps of the winter chill,
Like the presence of a general,
The plants and animals stand at command,
Awoken from their deep sleep.
Green grass growing, baby birds chirping,
The image of peace, lost among the
Fallen comrade in the act of defiance;
Guns blazing, shells bursting, smashing
The once tranquil lands and throws them into ruin.
Friends and family, oblivious.
To the thoughts racing past their beloved's mind,
Sights seen passing through those once innocent eyes,
And drowning them amid the bloodshed.
Alas, the waking of the spring shall be forever postponed,
The revival of nature untold,
Forever the world shall be plunged into the darkness of the night,
Snatched by the bitter cold of frigid winter,
The fallen leaves turn to ash,
Like the collapse of peace crumbling from the world.
Those once cherished loved ones
With memories of past,
But only a plaguing thought in mind:
'Protect the peace'.

William Chen (14)
The Crypt School, Gloucester

Love's Entrapment

Denial has no desirable outcome,
For, I realise that as shoes are to feet
Moulded around you, this life has now become;
And fleeing achieves little: it causes the two to meet
Only resulting in myself becoming worn on the ground
In which your image is imprinted deeper onto my sole.
Yet, striving to win favour gains nought control,
How many rays has verdure flora ever stole?
Though on scraps the seedling does steadily rise,
Basking in you, your manner and radiance
And fickleness of youth this love defies,
Since even the leaves, with no loyal essence
Stay true to you when you depart causing night
Ignoring all the other faint lights.

Alas . . . logicality destroyed charming wild long ago
So what right, have I, to fertilise feeling's fallow?
When reactions can integrity remove
With pretext being based on scraping of shells
With nuclei not met making move
Impossible to clear result foretell.
Such stubborn striving surely shows men are not all the same,
As choosing perseverance depends on that the heart contains,
So perhaps it is flawed to follow other's laurels;
Since in Earth's core, there is oil plus water,
And wrong well, like course in love, does enfeeble.
I'll hold my tongue, only time can confer
A gift from you - flame - to let me ignite and suffuse with your crimson,
From which set alight we shall shine in celestial amalgamation.

James Robertson (17)
The Crypt School, Gloucester

Through Someone's Eyes

Through their eyes I see war
Guns and bombs exploding.

Through their eyes I see jealousy
Hurting people for no reason.

Through their eyes I see murder
Killing innocent people with daggers and guns.

Through their eyes I see theft
Taking things that don't belong to you.

Through their eyes I see disease
Killing anyone in its path.

Through their eyes I see prison
Where all bad people belong.

Through their eyes I see bad people
The people who don't deserve anything.

Through their eyes I see good people
The people who deserve more.

Nikolas Latham (12)
The Crypt School, Gloucester

Abandoned House

The dark and damp abandoned house
The really small squeaky mouse
The broken staircase full of holes
The really ancient religious scrolls
The flickering light bulb on the stairs
The bed duvet full of cat hairs
The living room window left wide open
The glass inside is all broken
Serves the owners right
Their buying budget was a bit tight.

Elias McGill (13)
The Crypt School, Gloucester

Six Weeks

Six weeks have come again
Six weeks of boredom, misery and pain.
I look into the clock upon this hour and think of what used to be.
My friends have gone to drugs and lure
Now there's nothing left for me.
For once again the time has come
For here it is six weeks has come.
Again six weeks of boredom, misery and pain
For six weeks I have to hide from gangs and drugs,
It makes me too scared to go outside.
For people who live on this estate today
There is no escape because of those that hurt and bully them.
They are tomorrow!

Rupert Milward-Wiffen (13)
The Crypt School, Gloucester

My World

I live in a world of imagination,
They call me the craziest boy in the nation.
In my world the sky is pink,
Blue is the floor, it's the way I think.

In my world I live in a wonky house,
With my pet green rhino and a mouse.
My mum is an alien from outer space,
She's got three antenna on her face.

The trees are made of cotton wool,
There's a giant bath as the swimming pool.
But now my world's about to shut,
Because I've got a bug inside my gut.

Aaron Messenger (13)
Wellsway School, Keynsham

It's Just Me

Another break time all alone,
With no company, not even a phone,
They will be here soon,
It's the same time every day,
Even though it hurts me,
It's 'Just a game we play'.

I have to stay there, not saying a word,
Knowing I'll be dead if anything gets heard.
One day it will be over,
This can't be my life,
Don't they have hearts?
Telling them it's not right?

And when it stops I'll make it clear,
Show them what it's like living in fear.
I want my revenge,
They've made me a 'Nobody',
One day I will . . .
I'll be a 'Somebody'.

Rhianna Place (13)
Wellsway School, Keynsham

The Rut

All's quiet on the isle of rum,
With the sea birds flying overhead.
When all peace is shattered with a loud bellow and roar
And over the hill he comes, huge antlers on his head.

The red deer stag is a mass of muscle
Trying to defend his does.
Other males trying to take his hot spot.
They are his very worst foes.

Another stag comes down to challenge.
They lower their heads ready to fight.
To win over all of the females,
They will use all of their muscle and might.

First the charge then the lock,
The obvious winner shone.
A change of tactics a quick sharp move.
And then the other stag has won.

And then the scene turns away,
With a new stag peace stands strong.
Now he can start mating in calm.
And nothing will go wrong.

Daniel Brady (12)
Wellsway School, Keynsham

Save Our Species

Swinging and leaping from tree to tree,
Jungle filled with screeches and chatter.
Picking fruits from above their heads.
The future of these monkeys really does matter.

Sneaking stealthily through the grass,
Growling, prowling, an almighty roar.
Tiger's fur blazing brightly,
But he doesn't know what lies in store.

Swooping, soaring among the clouds,
Dark eyes focused on its prey.
Eagle's claws as sharp as knives,
But he won't be hunting again one day.

Stampeding and stomping through thick undergrowth,
Creased like leather, rough grey skin.
Huge ears flapping and trunk flailing,
The problems for these elephants will soon begin.

Slow and gentle, black and white,
Fur as smooth as the softest velvet.
Panda's huge eyes searching for leaves,
Soon to be trapped in a hunter's net.

Senseless and cruel, caring just about wealth,
Selfish poachers, greedy and sly.
Take a moment to think what's happening,
Because we'll soon have to wave some species goodbye.

Angharad Gravell (13)
Wellsway School, Keynsham

Make Poverty History!

The crowds are here,
Everyone's arrived.
Quiet rehearsals backstage,
This show's going live!

The lights on stage flicker,
Lions' roars can be heard
People sing along to songs,
One voice tells the world.

Suddenly it's my turn,
The crowds are cheering loud.
Adrenaline's pumping through my head,
As I tell the screaming crowd.

These are my words, my words
And I believe in what I say.
Make poverty history, now,
Yes make poverty history now.

As I walk off stage,
I hear the crowd
Agreeing with what I say.
And I know they believe my words.

The end is near, the last
Songs echo far away.
A man goes on stage and
People listen to what he has to say.

I listen in as the crowds start to cheer
We've made poverty history!
Yes, we've made poverty history;
For now, anyway.

Emily Peters (13)
Wellsway School, Keynsham

Bang, Bang Went The Gun

Bang, bang went the gun,
Like an eagle; relaxed, easy,
Flying towards the innocent victim.

Bang, bang went the gun,
Men fall down; cries of agony fill the smoky air.
Friends mourn over dead bodies,
Helpless, waiting for the end.

Bang, bang went the gun,
Through no-man's-land the bullets fly.
Men against each other, fire in their eyes,
With a passion for their country and people.

Bang, bang went the gun,
Grief fills the air, flesh is torn apart.
Brothers die, fathers, sons give up the fight;
Never to go home again, never again to see their families.

Bang, bang went the gun,
Through the deserted land to meet its target.
The target, a boy, not yet grown,
Stands in the way, the brave soul,
To protect his men, his team.

Charlotte Miché (13)
Wellsway School, Keynsham

If They Could Talk

We cannot speak or shout out like you,
We cannot tell you when we're hurt.
You are superior
You are a killer
You just don't think that we are
Just like you.

Do you remember?
That if it wasn't for
Us, you wouldn't be here,
You evolved from me.

But you think you're special
Though you are really not.
Our brains are the same
So what makes you so special?

My name is not yours
Your home is not mine
But think about this when you're killing my kind,
Human and chimpanzee . . .
You're an animal like
Me.

Clare Gosling (13)
Wellsway School, Keynsham

We're Killing Ourselves

War and anger and hatred and pain,
From this evil, what do we gain?
Nothing it seems, nothing at all,
Yet we continue, to abuse and brawl.

Shark-attacks, drought, cancer and tsunamis,
All come naturally, natural armies.
But the biggest killer, the worst of all,
It's nasty and selfish, it's us; people!

We cause the most anger and hatred and pain,
From this what do we stand to gain?
To kill ourselves, our future generations,
To ruin and wreck and destroy our nations.

We have to spring clean; polish and shine,
But this isn't our average household grime.
It's dirtier, murkier, a million times worse!
It's our evil, it's our curse.

Jess Bonney (14)
Wellsway School, Keynsham

The Orphan

If I left here tomorrow, would you still remember me?
If I said I was coming back, would you wait for me?

No? Then you are no friend.

If I needed help, would you save me?
If you had to risk your life, would you help me?

No? Then you are no friend.

Do people care for you?
Do they help you?
Would they die to save you?

Yes? Then you are not me,
And you are not lonely.

George Nethercott (13)
Wellsway School, Keynsham

Darkness

Darkness. The shutters of life,
Like a curtain, blocking all light.
Founder of fear, destruction and death,
But still living brave it, seeking its truth.

It creeps up on creatures, covering secrets,
Hiding plots and plans,
It will help anybody, but not for long,
And when you least expect it.

But then when you think you're lost and alone,
And have almost given up hope.
The sun will come shining in peace and joy,
Showing the start of life and love.

Yet try as it might,
It cannot fight,
Darkness' night,
With only light.

Katherine O'Hanlon (12)
Wellsway School, Keynsham

Tears

Water streams down her face,
A never-ending flow of sadness.
Through the tears a glint of hope flickers imperceptibly,
But harsh fingers paw at the face begging to return to norm.
Cause of this sorrow is a secret.
A false smile plastered on as she soldiers on.
Her heart aches with pain as if she was cruelly depriving it,
Lack of food deprives the starving.
Lack of love deprives the soul.
But to me her life has only begun,
When the last tear of sorrow has silently spun.

Alice Mould (13)
Wellsway School, Keynsham

Titanic

Off it sailed,
Jolly and happy,
Everyone oblivious,
To the terror ahead.

To the terror ahead,
Dark and gloomy,
The boat will plummet,
To the seabed.

Sailing swiftly,
Smooth and silent,
They saw it too late,
No time to stop.

No time to stop,
Lives will be lost,
Innocent people,
Have done nothing wrong.

The iceberg grew,
Larger and larger,
It came into contact,
With the starboard side.

With the starboard side,
Painted a deep red,
Behind that wall,
People slept.

It gorged the boat,
The water spilled in,
Drowning crew,
The gates would not close.

A film was made,
Everybody knows,
The tragic story,
Of when the Titanic sank.

Madeleine Parish (12)
Wellsway School, Keynsham

The Dark Stranger

The dark stranger glides silently along the empty beach,
The cold foaming waves lapping gently at his sandy bare feet,
He stops and turns to face the horizon,
Just a black shape against the deserted grey backdrop.

Gulls swoop like paper aeroplanes overhead,
The dark stranger doesn't flinch, but
Stares on steadily, unblinking,
Expressionless and still.

A strong breeze gushes past out to sea,
But the dark stranger stays unmoving,
His silhouette like that of a statue,
Bold and imposing; mighty and unperturbed.

The dark stranger is always, and won't be never,
He follows the path of the water for eternity,
Tracing its footsteps, creating his own,
A haunting image etched into our minds forever.

Zoë Dashfield (13)
Wellsway School, Keynsham

What Would Happen If I didn't Exist?

What would happen if I didn't exist?
Would I have closed my eyes like this?
Would I curl up and never speak,
For even longer than ten thousand weeks?

What would happen if I was invisible?
I know that I'm barely visible.
If I had my last day now,
At least people wouldn't look at me so foul.

What would happen if I didn't exist?
At least I wouldn't be cold like this.
So while the world carries on its play,
I will quietly, slip away.

Diana Brain (13)
Westonbirt School, Tetbury

Where The Wild Things Are

Let us go, you and me
To where the wild things are . . .
Where trees are not trees and paths are not paths
And happiness seems a thing of the past
And terror and jealousy rule over all
And the flowers and birds grow incredibly small
And the world seems to spin at quadruple the speed
Situations around you continue to feed
The despair.

Let us go, me and you
To this terrible place
Where the panic you show in your paleness of face
Is minute when compared to internal distress
When you realise that one day you too will digress.
But just try turning back. Do you dare? Do you dare?
As we all know that life can be truly unfair
But the most unfair thing is that some day you'll find
That you'll never escape - you are trapped.

By your mind.

Lucy Clare (16)
Westonbirt School, Tetbury

In The Shadows

The wind blew fiercely a slight tinge of silver in the air
The clouds swung etched with rays of glittering darkness
Gloom and death lingered pedestrians on a crossing
The door of the shed 'creaked' open the carcass
Of his body left to rot
'What have you done to him?' the man shouted
Emerging from the shadows
He ran to the shed
And was never seen again.

Vicky Butcher (12)
Westonbirt School, Tetbury

Looking Through The Castle's Eyes

Roses like bunches of balls,
Rosy-red standing tall,
A yew tree standing up,
Into the sky,
Flower buds like twisting gold wire,
Tough green leaves like waxy candles,
Spread open like a giant's hand,
Wispy grass swaying in the wind,
Honeysuckle like spiders' legs,
Babascum as tall as a dog on his hind legs,
Clematis twisting up a lush green bush,
Two-tone ivy creeping up the wall,
Berberis - its tall purple leaves,
Shimmering in the sunlight,
The flag flies fluttering on the flag pole,
The red bricks,
Sandstone red,
The drainpipe carefully carved,
But now it has been worn over the years,
Weathervane,
Shimmering coal-black,
Arch shape windows,
With emblems and shields painted on them,
Arrow slit windows,
Ready for someone to shoot out of,
The copper roof,
Grass like green,
I can see all this,
I am the castle.

Harriet Smith (12)
Westonbirt School, Tetbury

The Fair

All the clowns gathering in,
Tripping over bin by bin,
Over the ceiling, over the hedge,
I wonder what's going to come up next.

The house is on fire,
They all have a hose,
Can I tell you a secret,
They do have a big nose.

Next comes in the acrobats,
Swinging over, stealing hat by hat,
The clowns get the 'clown's fire brigade',
I get the hysterics until I turn white and fade.

Then come in the lions roaring so loudly,
Now it's not so funny,
I know they're quite tame,
But I'm still terrified,

And now it's over . . .

I had a fantastic time!

Rosie Poole (11)
Westonbirt School, Tetbury

Young Writers Information

We hope you have enjoyed reading this book - and that you will continue to enjoy it in the coming years.

If you like reading and writing poetry drop us a line, or give us a call, and we'll send you a free information pack.

Alternatively if you would like to order further copies of this book or any of our other titles, then please give us a call or log onto our website at www.youngwriters.co.uk

**Young Writers Information
Remus House
Coltsfoot Drive
Peterborough
PE2 9JX**

(01733) 890066